At one point in this heart-rending story, Zoe reflects on a line from Kahlil Gibran, 'Only great sorrows or great joy can reveal the truth.' *From Hardship to Hope* gives us an abundance of sorrow, joy, and truth. And a heaping amount of hope. Co-authors Adrian and Stueber have teamed up to create a powerful story that is as relevant as today's headlines and as time worn as all matters of the heart. Hope is their superpower.

—Doug Bradley, author, educator, veteran

From Hardship to Hope offers a glimpse into what our community could be if, like Ruby Blue and Zoe, we take a chance on someone else. It's a reminder of what can happen to our hearts and lives when we are willing to engage with one another (and ourselves), honestly, authentically, and from a place of love. Stueber and Adrian move the reader from hardship to hope through the telling of four different love stories. Upon finishing this book, I was reminded of these words from 1 Corinthians: 'And now these three remain, faith, hope, and love. But the greatest of these is love.'

—Linda Ketcham, Executive Director,
Madison-area Urban Ministry (dba JustDane)

From Hardship to Hope provides a real-world reflection on America today. Civil unrest, racism, poverty, ageism, discrimination, gender inequality, oppression, COVID, and so much more. As a Black male and father raising a young Black daughter and son, the worries and concerns I have for them in this world are overwhelming. Thinking about the 'Talk' I will have with them about how people will look at them and treat them differently, just because of the pigmentation of their skin. I hope they will grow up in a much different world, where people realize that we are all humans and more connects us than separates us."

—Dr. Derek L. Johnson

From Hardship to Hope by Judith Gwinn Adrian and Jaylin M. Stueber spins a touching story of honesty, learning, and compassion, weaving truth and fiction into a what-if tale reminiscent of John Lennon's "Imagine." Seen through the lens of a global pandemic, the authors comment on social issues including discrimination, social justice, teen pregnancy, and a variety of ills challenging life in the early 2020s. Their vision of what could be is an invitation worth consideration."

—Susan A. Marshall
Founder, Backbone Institute, LLC
"Never grow a wishbone where a backbone ought to be."

One powerful story. Of redemption and reconciliation, recovery and discovery. On page after page, another reminder—sometimes gentle, other times jarring—of how little we know each other but how much we share in common. Amazing how two lives can be glaringly unequal yet eerily similar, utterly disconnected for years, suddenly intertwined, bonded for good, stronger than the forces that partition us in this day and age.

—Mike McCabe, Farm-raised writer, social justice advocate, and democracy defender

In *From Hardship to HOPE*, Judith Adrian and Jaylin Stueber eloquently illustrate conflicting human emotions that life's journey can give rise to: joy and anger, happiness and sadness, trust and distrust, love and antipathy, despair and hope. The authors demonstrate compelling, often disturbing, incidents of racial profiling and injustices that, as a nation, we need to work harder to "right the wrongs" in today's world. This compelling book is a must read!!!

—Kathy Sweeney, Retired Operating Room Nurse

Adrian and Stueber have come together to deliver a story that embraces the richness of relationship in a time of crisis...A message of discovery that in its subtle intensity introduces us to the power of relationship, connecting the unknown, to the known ability of the human capacity for growth-this is where the inability to see the "other," begins to implode and births the richness of empathy and understanding. Adrian and Stueber have gracefully given us a lifeline that centers-creates the space where the need to unlearn brings balance to the human soul.

—James Morgan Former Peer Trainer and Specialist, JustDane, Madison, WI

I read the manuscript as a Black woman with professional lived experiences in the criminal justice system and higher education. And personally, as a mother and grandmother of Black female-born persons who all love Black men.

Thus, so many of my intersectional identities were captivated by the lived experiences of both Ruby Blue and Zoe. As a proud Black woman who has lived, unapologetically, over half of my life, I consistently resonated with the stories shared. I appreciated the authors' commitment to connecting the wisdom of those who have come before us to contemporary voices (even those abruptly silenced) who bring the necessary combination of deep understanding and a resolute call to action for equity. #realmeetsreal

—Pearl Leonard-Rock, DEI Consultant at UW Health
and the UW School of Medicine and Public Health

At a time when people, even people of good will, too often seem to be living in different universes, Hardship to Hope achieves something rare and precious. Zoe and Ruby Blue come from different places, perceive the world through different lenses, but through a series of sometimes painful, sometimes perplexing conversations, create a shared vision that offers a model for moving ahead into a world where we can be together without being the same.

—Craig Werner, author of *A Change Is Gonna Come:
Music, Race & the Soul of America*

A warm and touching read about two very different women brought together unexpectedly and unwillingly. This story takes us through their journey of discovery, healing and building trust and reminds us all of the power of love, understanding and compassion.

—Shawn Johnson, Career Coach/Program Manager
– Wisconsin School of Business

The book *From Hardship to Hope* tells a powerful story as it depicts the lived experiences of two women from completely different worlds. With preconceived opinions about the other, both women were challenged to overcome their own biases and prejudices. From being fearful of the other person because of the intersectionality of their individual identities to forming a meaningful relationship, the story of Ruby Blue and Zoe illustrates the power of inter-cultural and cross-cultural dialogue. The ways in which Ruby Blue and Zoe cared for one another is remarkable and provides a sense of hope that each and every one of us can make a difference in the lives of others, no matter their background or identity. The story also reminds us that despite the challenges of our society, there are still kind-hearted people in this world. As this book emphasizes, "We are all one being, just different. Human. Being."

—Dr. Derek L. Johnson

From Hardship to Hope, Judith Gwinn Adrian & Jaylin M. Stueber. Two women on different ends of the spectrum in terms of race, age, and awareness come together to trust, respect, and learn from each other.
—Branden Mead, Coordinator and Success Coach at Madison College for Teens of Promise + (TOPS+)

From Hardship to Hope teems with the love and challenges faced by two women who have experienced being pregnant teenagers.

As an adoptee, I appreciate Adrian and Stueber's honesty in describing the uphill battle that young, unwed pregnant mothers face; a battle marked by shame when Zoe was a young woman and by the institutional racism encountered by Ruby Blue. Ruby Blue's description of her narrowing choices are vivid and yet her determination and sense of history point her forward and connect to her late Granny, whose love she manifests when her own daughter is born. Zoe's searing description of being sequestered by her family in a home for unwed pregnant mothers in Texas and the cold, clinical birthing of her son sheds light on an experience that is rarely described.

Despite their commonalities as women, Ruby Blue and Zoe have vastly different experiences of race and ideas about racism. The realizations about racism that Zoe comes to are sometimes awkward and cringe-worthy, but her willingness to look at herself and try to understand what it means to be a young woman of color is laudable. Ruby Blue, faced with Zoe's Midwestern stalwartness and kindness, also examines her misconceptions of white people and eventually finds an ally in Zoe.
—Nancy K. Fishman, writer and adoptee

This book shows us how separations can be bridged. At the start, the two women could not be farther apart. How is this great divide crossed?

It's done through hard work, openness, fate, and love. It is wonderful storytelling. This is a blockbuster of a book. It can teach us!
—Carol Lobes, Former Director of Dane County Human Services

What happens when two women who seem to have nothing in common except distrust of each other are suddenly thrown together as housemates during the pandemic? The initial situation sounds unlikely, but the authors make it plausible. They also made me care about both Zoe and Ruby Blue as they gradually overcome their initial misconceptions, cope with their own losses, and learn to appreciate and protect each other. The book's title promises hope, but it delivers even more. I'd call it an inspiring story of kindness, courage, and unexpected love. Highly recommended!

—Sherry Reames, Emeritus Professor of English, UW–Madison

I loved how both of the main characters started uncomfortable and challenged in their relationship but chose to say rather than walk away. They soon moved from focusing on their differences to embracing their similarities. In turn, their love for each other grew. A beautiful reminder to embrace proximity.

—Cheryl McNamee, Patient Services Director at First Care Clinic

From
HARDSHIP
to
HOPE

Crossing the great divides of age, race,
wealth, equity, and health

Other books by and with Judith Gwinn Adrian:

**Pauly, Diane Wallner & Judith Gwinn Adrian (2022). *A Purpose-Driven Life of Helping Others*. Milwaukee: HenschelHAUS.

**Rodriguez, Pascual & Judith Gwinn Adrian (2022). *Rounding Third and Finally Home*. Milwaukee: HenschelHAUS,

**Clauer, Joshua William & Judith Gwinn Adrian (2022). *Walking the Line: There is No Time for Hate*. Milwaukee: HenschelHAUS.

**Adrian, Judith Gwinn (March 2020). *Nancer the Dancer: Myositis and Me*. Milwaukee: HenschelHAUS. (Reader's Choice – five stars)

**Adrian, Judith Gwinn (February 1, 2019). *Tera's Tale*. Milwaukee: HenschelHAUS. (March 2019 Finalist, Eric Hoffer/Montaigne Medal)

**Adrian, Judith Gwinn & DarRen Morris (2014). *In Warm Blood: Prison, Privilege, Hurt, & Heart*. Milwaukee: HenschelHAUS. (USA BOOK AWARDS: 2015 finalist in non-fiction, Multi-cultural and True Crime categories)

**Millar, Jackie & Judith Gwinn Adrian (2007, 2010). Because I Am Jackie Millar. Los Angeles: Golden: The Press.

**Lawton, Rebecca & Dawn Rosewitz (2022). *Hernzebekana! Her Language of Love*. Milwaukee: HenschelHAUS. (editor)

From
HARDSHIP
to
HOPE

Crossing the great divides of age, race,
wealth, equity, and health

Judith Gwinn Adrian
and
Jaylin M. Stueber

Henschel
HAUS
Milwaukee, Wisconsin

Published by
HenschelHAUS Publishing, Inc.
www.henschelHAUSbooks.com
Milwaukee, Wisconsin

ISBN: 978159598-960-4
LCCN: 2023945778

Artwork and cover by Phil Salamone

Printed in the United States of America

Dedication

To the Black and Brown Youth who are no longer here
due to social injustices.

To all those who remain silent
because they don't have a platform to elevate their voices.

"Historically, pandemics have forced humans to break with the past and imagine their world anew. This one is no different. It is a portal, a gateway between one world and the next. We can choose to walk through it, dragging the carcasses of our prejudice and hatred, our avarice, our data banks and dead ideas, our dead rivers and smoky skies behind us. Or we can walk through lightly, with little luggage, ready to imagine another world. And ready to fight for it."
—Arundhati Roy

"An old world is dying, and a new one, kicking in the belly of its mother, time, announces that it is ready to be born. This birth will not be easy, and many of us are doomed to discover that we are exceedingly clumsy midwives. No matter, so long as we accept that our responsibility is to the newborn: the acceptance of responsibility contains the key."
—James Baldwin

*"There will be a new killing today.
It just ain't happen' yet."*
—Jaylin M. Stueber

This is a book of autofiction, a writing that combines two seemingly inconsistent narrative forms: autobiography and fiction.

In this instance, we have combined two people's stories, two lives connected through lived experience, coupled through fictional threads.

FOREWORD

Among the many responses to the history-altering Covid pandemic has been a need to explain, to ourselves and each other, what it meant; truly, deeply meant, in the ways it changed us forever. A growing number of writers have posited their explanations. But few have told the story of the inextricably intertwined influences of Covid, political turmoil, and the historic acknowledgement of social injustice with the self-aware introspection, unapologetic honesty, and remarkably successful shared perspective of Judith Gwinn Adrian and Jaylin M. Stueber's fictionalized autobiography *From Hardship to Hope*.

This is a risky book. Co-authorship is always complicated, and Adrian and Stueber have clearly pushed each other to some uncomfortable places. But the result is a provocative, at times difficult, but ultimately deeply rewarding story of lives intertwined and yes, changed forever.

Another byproduct of Covid is that we are drawn to relate to others with experiences similar to ours. Adrian and Stueber pull us into shared experiences of confusion, fear, anxiety, stoic acceptance, determination, human mistakes, and extra human courage we didn't know we had. We see ourselves in the lives of wise, olding, relentlessly introspective Dr. Zoe Smyth, who "believed she knew what the hell she was about," and street-smart, brash yet vulnerable Ruby Blue, who "thought I was pretty basic," seeing the world through the eyes of both herself and her unborn daughter. Self images that for both women will be reimagined and redefined, as will our own.

Adrian and Stueber, like Zoe and Ruby Blue, push, prod, irritate, and delight each other and both give us the benefit of two voices; those that speak out loud and those that speak to themselves, sometimes complementary, sometimes conflicting. We also hear the voices of ever-present Fred, Zoe's still supportive, sustaining, late husband, and "irresistible" Marcus, Ruby Blue's incarcerated "King" and baby's father. We even hear from the virus itself.

The voices of *From Hardship to Hope* comprise a meditation on age, career, love, race, and difference, with the patience of experience, the urgency and passion of youth, and with the isolation and creeping loneliness of quarantine, the division and separation of politics, and the ardent fervor of demands for social justice denied: four lives, richly detailed, so different, so similar, and of course the fifth life that keeps drawing us to hope.

Ruby Blue and Zoe's essential philosophical journey from "Hardship to Hope" challenges our epistemology. What do we really know? How do we square our beliefs and our opinions with our knowledge? All from life experiences as different as "the streets," "the rez," the ivory tower of academia, and the caste system in India. It has the feeling of an ancient story of human connection told in language and a context as contemporary as this moment.

Like one of Zoe and Ruby Blue's conversations, our experience reading the book warms and cools, warms again, a little uncomfortably, until one of the two deftly turns down the heat before it reaches a boiling point. In the process, they, and we, contemplate real poverty, the experience of incarceration, sex, pregnancy, child-birth, adoption, and compare traumas and the strongboxes in our chests in a Covid-infected world.

Adrian and Stueber expose, no, explode the tension of literature and story vs. lived experience. And weren't we all, like Zoe and Ruby Blue, gobsmacked by the wonder, the mystery in the surreal existence of the crazy virus. Only now are we telling ourselves, and each other, that somehow there also emerged new knowledge, genuine compassion, authentic generosity of spirit and ultimately, out of all the hardship, hope. Because "realness recognizes realness," as Ruby Blue tells us. Thanks to Adrian's and Stueber's realness we recognize a path to realness for ourselves.

—Neil Heinen
Writer and journalist

PREFACE

From Hardship to Hope invites us to walk into the complexities of two women's parallel universes. It is a fictionalized, shared autobiography. Some of the moments and experiences come from Jaylin's and Judith's lives. Some do not.

* * *

Ruby Blue, a pregnant, homeless, Black teen is temporarily housed with Zoe, a White, olding widow, as Covid-19 disrupts their lives.

Their daily pace slows and after a stormy start, Zoe and Ruby Blue begin to build trust, sharing increasingly insightful life experiences as they stay together. Zoe knows her world through books and travel. Ruby Blue knows her world through life on the streets.

At the same time the pandemic clouds the pace of life, the Black Lives Matter movement roils out of the unrest and the inequalities—laid bare by Covid-19—showcasing differences in job prospects, educational possibilities, housing opportunities, health care access, and societal transformation. Together, the women struggle with these realities.

Over time, Zoe and Ruby Blue share their defining stories. And some secrets. They talk about family differences in favorite foods, hair styles, skin care, and history. (The women have the same last name, with different spellings.) Then, carefully, yet often bluntly, they compassionately move to discussing tough topics, each from her own background. Race. Age. Gender. Poverty. Healthcare. Pregnancy. Adoption. Protesting. Policing. Incarceration. Death. Trust. Love.

Singer H.E.R. raises the question of how people can look at exactly the same event or entity and come away with opposite interpretations. She asks, can the killer and the protector be the same person, an idea the women deliberate.

From Hardship to Hope challenges us to consider where our—often strongly held—different beliefs and assumptions about reality come from.

How did each of us learn to see the world as we do? Zoe clings to her heritage through her grandmother's sugar bowl and striped chair. Ruby Blue pulls her incarcerated man's blue hoodie tightly around her distended belly.

How do we dare to question these realities we so strongly believe? Ruby Blue's lived experiences tell her to fear the police—the "pigs," as she calls them. Zoe tells of the time a police officer saved her from a predator, to which Ruby Blue asks, *Why did you call him a predator?*

How do we come to see that our understanding is ultimately subjective, that other people authentically experience different realities? Hold different truths. The women's experiences of giving birth—objectively the same event—could not have been more divergent.

David McRaney, in *How Minds Change: The Surprising Science of Belief, Opinion, and Persuasion*, suggests that true contact changes minds. True means meeting (in situations of equal status), sharing common goals, cooperating to meet those goals, engaging in informal interactions, and recognizing and addressing the concerns each person holds. Zoe and Ruby Blue were able to meet each of these reckonings.

And then, ultimately, what do we do with our new understandings? Can we come away with hope, as these women were able to do.

JUDITH

My journey into wanting to understand racial, economic, and privilege differences began after my father, a physician and medical researcher, told me he had been incarcerated. Although this was a shock, I was too caught up in my own teenage angst to try to understand the implications of this until much later, after both he and my mother were long gone.

As part of my University of Wisconsin–Madison graduate studies, I was lucky enough to work with Jerold Apps, both as his advisee and as a project assistant. The project was the National Extension Leadership Development program, funded by the Kellogg Foundation, with the intent of deepening leadership skills within the Cooperative Extension System, nationwide. A central tenet of the program, as it was conceived, was diversity. My job was to make connections in communities the "interns" would travel to during their two-year involvement. Over four years, we took groups to Fort Berthold Indian Reservation; Tuskegee, Alabama; Mexico City, and Western Europe. The interns, and their stories, were the gist of my dissertation. The richness. I learned so much from them and their life experiences.

After graduation, I wanted to delve more deeply into understanding what my father's incarceration had meant to our family. While teaching, I met a woman, Jackie Millar, who came to speak to one of my graduate classes. I asked her if she and I could write her story of having been shot, execution style, by two boys, 15 and 16 years old, and then left for dead.

She had survived and begun teaching about forgiveness. She said no to writing her story because it would be too traumatizing for her sons to relive it all.

A year later, she changed her mind and said yes, and that became my first book, *Because I am Jackie Millar*. I had asked her how she was able to forgive the boys who left her paralyzed on half of her body, legally blind, and cognitively impaired. Her answer? *I forgive because it is who I am; I do this because I am Jackie Millar.*

As we spent a year together, going to prisons and jails and juvenile detention centers where she so slowly spoke about forgiveness, I saw a common theme. Even in Wisconsin and Michigan and Minnesota, the prisoners and detainees were predominantly Black or Brown. Why?

I decided to go more deeply into prison, so joined a ministry program that visited maximum security prisons every Friday, for two-hour conversations with prisoners. It was there I met DarRen Morris. I asked him if we could write his life story and he said no.

After three years of meeting weekly with the circle of prisoners and the ministry team, DarRen grew to trust me and said yes to the book. Together we wrote his back story, the events of his crime, and his life sentence received when he was 17 years old. *In Warm Blood: Prison & Privilege, Hurt & Heart* is a compilation of his story and my awakening to the depth of the White privilege I had lived with and accepted as my due.

Publisher Kira Henschel was taking manuscripts at this time so I sent her DarRen's and my book. She read it and said she would publish it. That moment began a joyful and auspicious relationship that has taken me into the world of writing memoirs—some on my own and some with co-writers.

The idea for *From Hardship to Hope*—Zoe and Ruby Blue's story—emerged during the weighty years of the Covid-19 pandemic when many people's daily patterns changed and our world shuddered on its axis. There were three dovetailed triggers.

First was a photo of the child's image, now painted by Phil Salamone, that became the cover design. I thought, and think, that she is the most captivating child I have ever seen. She is the future.

Second was the actual plea for temporary housing for a homeless teen, printed in a local community newspaper. That became the fictionalized link that initially brought Zoe and Ruby Blue together.

And third was the Black Lives Matter protests—and sadly some riots—shown daily in TV news broadcasts, coming out of inequities laid bare by the pandemic. Partly as a result of the protests, cable TV stations began playing movies and documentaries about African American life experiences. Free. I watched these and also read many books about these same experiences as a result of both the opportunity and the extraordinary times. Mail delivery through Amazon.com provided the books—some new, some used—at a time when the libraries were closed for months.

As I watched and read, I kept a list of words and phrases that depicted Black English—African American Vernacular English (AAVE)—to me. I knew I could not accurately portray Ruby Blue's words and attitude, but gave it a try in the first book draft.

During this time, I was part of a Circle of Support for a returning prisoner, a formerly incarcerated woman. The weekly support talks were conducted via Zoom, as was much else during the pandemic. It was through that Circle of Support that I met Jaylin Stueber, who was working as a manager at a functioning car wash while also completing her master's degree.

As the pandemic eased, we were together at an outdoor picnic, celebrating the work with returning prisoners and their families. I had seen Jaylin's chutzpa and caring from the earlier Circle, so invited her to co-write the book with me. She said no.

A year later, when our paths again crossed and I was still working on fine-tuning the no-name book, she said yes.

And so, we began.

We learned that our best way of jointly reading the manuscript was to use the "Read Aloud" function in Microsoft Word. We listened to the book. Some days twenty pages at a time. Some days less.

Regularly (and I mean regularly!) Jaylin would make comments on language, on depth of setting and scene, on the direction of the story and, most importantly, on the ending, which I had not yet figured out as I debated about who in the story would live and who might die. (I did realize that with a baby as compelling as Marca Hope on the cover, the baby could not die in this fictionalized story.)

The book and the story are hugely improved because of Jaylin's input. I am deeply grateful! We are genuinely co-creators of Zoe and Ruby Blue's story, *From Hardship to Hope*.

JAYLIN

The moment I found out I was an outsider was when I transferred to the University of Wisconsin–Madison. I was blind to the amount of Whiteness in Dane County. Growing up, I had been around Black, Brown, and White kids.

Reality sucker-punched me while being enrolled at the university. Although I am bi-racial, to the teachers and students, I was only Black. And, let me tell you, I was not prepared for that experience at all. It was sickening, but somehow, I found a home in the School of Social Work. Everywhere else on campus, I was just this Black student no one wanted to sit by, talk to, study with, or even engage with during class time. They acted as if I was not supposed to be there. Like I was lost and didn't belong. There were even moments I would cry because I felt I wasn't worthy of the Badger experience. But then I would snap out of my funk and tell myself there is clearly a reason I was supposed to be there and I was just as smart as any other student on that campus. Most importantly, through this experience, I became firm in, and proud of, my identity as a Black woman.

When Judith came to me about writing the book the first time, I was on-board to edit and provide feedback from my bi-racial perspective. But I was not invested in writing. To be honest, I never saw myself as an author, so didn't see a need to help write this book. Ultimately, I backed out because life got in the way and the project became too overwhelming.

However, somehow, she got me y'all and I said yes.

What changed my mind was that I felt badly because it is rare that I don't finish things that I've started. I really liked the manuscript and I realized that while reading it again, I had to help this White lady because she was about to get cussed out by a lot of Black readers. Naïvely, she made us sound like old slaves and that's just not right. Reading through the manuscript, I began to see myself in this Ruby Blue character. I could see her strengths and struggles, and although they are not identical to mine, I realized I could work with this. Once I allowed myself to be open-minded, I was like, "Yeah, let's do this." Who better than me to provide expertise on someone who is smart in both the books and the streets.

Overall, this has been a really awesome experience because I got to express myself in a way I've never done before. In a way, I got to tell my story, without really telling my story, because I had the mask of a character. The only way you'd know this is if you know me, or know Judith. This is a fun aspect of story-telling because I get to tell my truth in my own words.

Something I noticed throughout this project was that as our characters grew, so did we. Why? Because their growth allowed us to learn from each other, particularly through our more uncomfortable conversations.

It was hard to write together at times because we are both passionate about our stories and sometimes it is difficult to hear the other person out when it is your truth. Sometimes we went back and forth about edits and it made me worried because it took time to change things. I also did not realize how time-consuming this would be while I was trying to balance my own life with school and work and relationships and, most importantly, it cut into my "me" time. I would say that in the end, it was worth it, because there are sections of the book that I don't think we could have completed because it might not have happened if we had not been so firm in our stance. It was a Catch 22, because even though it was frustrating, it also was a distraction from my reality when I was able to be immersed in writing the book.

It is important to remember, nothing in this life is easy. If it were, everybody would be doing it. I think that is why this process is so worth it. I'm so excited to get our book out there because I'm hoping this can be a tool (or a weapon) for those who are living these experiences. Now they have literature to back up their feelings and realities.

Authors Jaylin Stueber and Judith Gwinn Adrian

COMPLETELY ALONE

Sometimes a man gets himself in a tight spot and there ain't much he can do. Not up to him any longer. I don't give up on you even though you made some bad choices, my Marcus.

Marcus. Marcus? Nah. I forgot. I'm woke now. You're gone. You're in jail. Oh shit!

Ruby Blue pulls the threadbare blue blanket around her more tightly, then sits up awkwardly on the grimy couch where she has slept, rubbing her fingers together to get rid of something sticky and feeling like an unmade bed of a human.

Hate this couch. It is a good thing I can't sleep on my stomach, with the baby and all, 'cause I don't want to breathe in the dirt; it ain't healthy. I have got to buck up. Why is it so quiet? Most of them are not usually sleepin' now.

Wrapped in the blanket, Ruby Blue opens the bedroom door and shuffles down the hallway, where the smell of smoke loiters, shoving an empty pizza box to the side with her toe.

Quiet. Just too quiet.

The only sounds are muffled voices from daytime TV and the neighbors—next apartment over—fighting, again. The living room and kitchen are littered with empty plastic grocery store bags, shards of shriveled pizza crust, a single flowered child's sock, broken plastic hangers in pastel colors, and fast-food containers with drips of BBQ sauce dried on the sides. It appears there is a path carved through the clutter, guiding her eyes toward the exit, the apartment door.

> *My...my...my. I thought I was pretty basic but now see I'm so dumb it'd take me an hour to cook Minute Rice. Guess I ain't got no good sense. I wouldn't do 'em like this. Gone. They all gone. Yeah, we're mad now. Wait?*

Ruby Blue twists and quickly returns to the bedroom, looking for her backpack.

> *The stimulus relief debit cards. Mine and Marcus'. Gone. They took my money. Our money. Nah, I'm not playin'.*

All that's left in the bedroom is Marcus' hoodie. Ruby Blue drops the blanket for the moment and slowly puts on his sweatshirt. It is too large but she pulls it tightly around her distended body, recalling the scent of him.

> *Alone. We are completely alone in this world. My baby and me—well, a pregnant woman is never actually alone. But we gotta focus on our feet—keep 'em movin'. Take control of what we can. No time for tears. I will call the 2-1-1 Helpline. Maybe there is room in a temporary shelter for me.*

Judith Guinn Adrian / Jaylin M Stueber

ZOE

ZOE

I wasn't always old. A distraction some call *life* turned my head, surprising me. This, however, is more observation than complaint. "Olding" is actually entertaining in its own odd way with its ruminations that don't reliably lead to serenity. Who knew?

Now, wrinkled, gnarled, and desexualized, I visualize myself liquifying, watching the rhythmic blue pulse when my hands are still. No question I'm invisible to most people, even though the pulsing in my veins infers life.

A still dignified, withering creature, I am blandly Midwestern and genetically British. I do know how to sit with grace, one leg behind the other to lower myself into a seated position, gently as a flutter, sitting with decorum and gentility. Whether erect posture is useful at my age is questionable, but it is a carryover; taught as one of my parents' many family-honored decrees.

Don't get me wrong. I love my hands, my relatively strong legs, and reasonably viable body. These parts are old, trusted friends that can still stand tall, albeit slowly, and will never be this *young* again. Many of my wrinkles slope inward to amiable spaces—from a habit of smiling over the years—when I knew how to turn teaching and learning into an engaging game and honored the truth that we are all teachers and all learners.

I thought I was aware of the privileges that came my way, some earned but many unearned. Over the years, writing many an academic grant proposal, I spouted evidence-based buzz words describing human differences, like race/ethnicity, Eurocentrism, language, citizenship, physical ability, gender identity, sexual orientation, beauty, arrest record, formal education, accessibility, poverty, emotional ability, socioeconomic class, religion, marital status, and on and on. But, as I was soon to be taught, I was surprisingly naïve in thinking I understood these terms, while not fully seeing how my narrow experience had framed my grasp of the larger world.

I was Dr. Smyth, a woman who believed she knew what the hell she was about. I was never one of those teachers, as the joke goes, who spoke while others slept. Student immersion was priority number one. Personal engagement. Involvement. Community.

Now, since retirement, I'm simply *Zoe*. I have learned not to bother about a crease or a spot on my shirt. No one knows, or cares, that in my previous life I taught literature and traveled much of the world—sometimes with students, sometimes with my husband, Fred. Curious I am, yes, with a hint of adventure.

Decades ago, I married Fred. A wise man for whom hands-on meant hands-in the dirt. Large hands that radiated warmth and smelled of raw earth. He taught agrarian ideas on the rez, respectfully learning as much as he taught. Fred, Fred, Fred.

My life mantra is: *there are many right ways*. And for us, our pragmatic marriage pattern was to teach at colleges separated by 1,000 miles, one of us in the arts and one in the sciences. We spent holidays together for twenty-five years and shared many delights. Perhaps such distancing is one edict for preserving long-term love. Our almost nomadic lifestyles meant we chose not to bring children into our marriage.

Recently, we had both retired to our house and were discovering how to live together, more like conventional marrieds.

Then Fred got sick. Covid. The evil virus that aggressively encircled the planet for more than two years. Why weren't we humans aware that a pandemic could happen in modern times? Naïve? Arrogant? Or maybe just too busy doing, doing, doing, to ponder this possibility.

Judith Guinn Adrian / Jaylin M Stueber

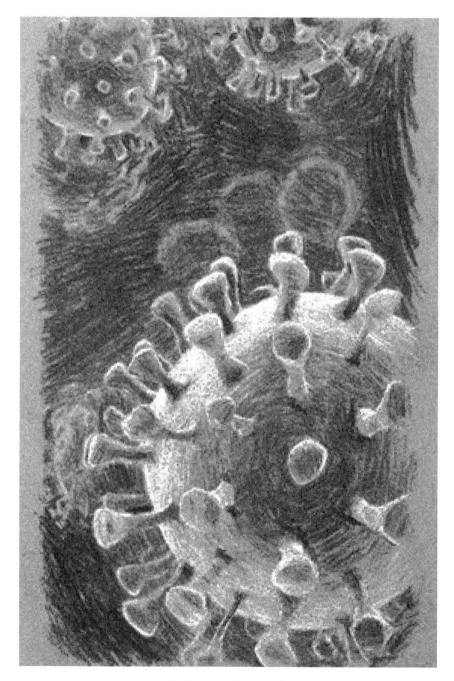

COVID-19

COVID-19

I am the virus. Let me work.

You are my victim. Just a fleeting look.

Transmissible with a capital T.

Yes, I am the monster. Mystery.

Shelter-in-place. Socially distance. Contact trace. Hoard toilet paper. Wash your groceries, then leave 'em outside. Soap your hands for 20 seconds, while humming the full measure of *Happy Birthday.*

Don't touch your eyes, nose, or mouth. Wear that mask. Gaiter up, so manly. Uh, over your mouth, nose, and, sure, playfully cover your eyes or neck.

Vulnerable elders are easiest: pre-existing conditions and whatnot. Add those with scarce resources; certain zip codes. Essential workers. Americans of every hue and Tuskegee-infused medical doubt.

The young ones? Closed schools. Empty classrooms. Kids playing hooky, except they are not playing. Loneliness. Depression. Lacking confidence. Lacking social connections.

- "I sat alone at home and at one in the morning went and bought a six-pack. The cashier didn't even card me because it was one in the morning and I looked sad."

- In the traffic-hush, white-crowned sparrows, and others, began to sing more quietly.

Tell 'em. I am a hoax. A ruse. A joke. Protest against reason; ignore science (but come running to it when your lungs shut down).

I am the virus. Support my aspirations.

Vaccines? The jab. No worries. Pretend vaccinating is an individual choice, not a team sport. Tell them. Tell 'em they will become stone people with generational altered DNA. Tell 'em Big Pharma is a liar. Tell 'em I'm a Wuhan biological-weapon. Tell 'em to drink bleach. Tell 'em I slither through 5-G networks.

I giggle. I am the virus.

- "What types of jokes are allowed during quarantine? Inside jokes."
- "If I had only known in March it would be my last time in a restaurant, I'd have ordered dessert."
- "The dumbest thing I ever purchased was a 2020 planner."
- "Ran out of toilet paper and started using lettuce leaves. Today was just the tip of the iceberg; tomorrow *romaines* to be seen."
- "Keep in mind, even during a pandemic, no matter how much chocolate you eat, your earrings will still fit."

I laugh at your brave little attempts. I am THE virus.

SARS, MERS, step aside. I can morph. Herd immunity? Like I said, I am a shape-shifter. Yes, I am the monster.

Ebola, rabies, poxviruses. Yes, all of us interacting with the environment and animals in new and unanticipated ways. Mosquitoes? My best friends. It is OUR time. And all y'all aren't learning. Add fungi...just the tip of another berg.

Six million gone in two years, and counting. Heart disease and cancer, step aside.

Number one. My aspiration is to be number one! The U.S., my biggest success. More than two decades of car crashes. More dead than on all the U.S. battlefields. Combined. Keep 'em coming.

- "Yes, wish we could talk, kiss, and hug. They are saying they will intubate me. Hate it in this ICU. I don't want to die alone."

- Those jails and prisons are porous. Staff in. Staff out. "Our priority during this public health crisis is the safety and health of Department of Corrections staff and persons in our care."

- They wheeled her toward the delivery room. She cried out in pain, "Don't leave me, don't leave me."

I am the virus. I force isolation, jam supply chains, cause inflation, create the great job resignation, spike unemployment, inflame civil unrest, initiate book bans, ramp up fear, excite depression, disrupt travel, destabilize the globe!

Traumatize.

Who knew it was all so fragile? Who knew I could create *Brigadoon*—a place that exists in a universe parallel to what had been normal life.

Yes, please, skip the vaccine. Fear the needle.

Pile 'em high. Shovel 'em under.

I am the virus. Years I steal.

Thanks for the support. It's been real.

MADE REDUNDANT

This pandemic was the real deal. One clue was the jokes: Why did they call it the *novel coronavirus*? It's a long story....get it? A novel. A story. A thriller!

Its true name is SARS-CoV-2, dubbed Covid-19 for the year, 2019, it was discovered. An unknown, but snarling disease. Our lives stopped on a dime, possibly a quarter, in mid-March of 2020, bringing Fred and me to dead-lock. Who knew that was literally going to be true. Our students? Sent home to isolate. Our jobs? Halted and then made redundant, which is unfriendly shorthand for, "Your services are subsequently unrequired."

> *Twenty-five years of dedication to an institution that, in a breath, says goodbye to a quarter of the faculty. If nothing is right with you in college, just go left. A liberal's joke. But that is what we literally did. We left.*

Younger faculty taught online. For Fred, teaching hands-in-the-dirt, it was close to impossible via *Blackboard* or *Zoom*. We were old dogs biting at the tires of new tricks. And crashing. Cutting us loose meant cost savings for our institutions. Tenure be damned in the crisis. Luckily, we had—well, practical Fred had—saved retirement funds. We also had our tiny, dated but ecological, house. Now our sacred space.

Fred and I decided this new masked time was an opportunity for steady togetherness in ways we hadn't lived for decades. We were excited. True, lust was long extinguished, but we were affectionate and even occasionally held hands, after the initial two weeks of separation in our quarantine-pod, as they were calling it.

One of our shared tongue-in-cheek pacts was that, when the first of us died, the other would get the partner's body stuffed by a taxidermist and prop him (or me) up on the couch. Given there was so little to talk about with the Covid isolation and lack of any activities—beyond having groceries dropped into the back of the car by a courageous *essential worker* in drive-through fashion—that degree of stuffed conversation might have been sufficient.

Fred and I married during the roil of the Vietnam war. In addition to sizzling sex in the back of his VW bug—a feat not to be scoffed at—we also appreciated each other intellectually. Some married students were given military deferments from the draft, so our hasty, nondescript wedding kept Fred safe. He was legitimately a college student as well, reportedly providing two protective layers of deferment from that ugly conflict. He was tough as a knot of pine and could have gone to war. But why go if you have a path out and genuinely do not believe in killing people, just because they have been assigned the label "enemy"? And marriage offered me a social acceptability that I shyly lacked following the lingering disgrace of my teenage pregnancy and the pain of having given a child up for adoption.

***

What piece of clothing might Fred have been? A wool sweater, warm but sometimes scratchy? Yes. Steel-toed work boots, effective but not fashionable? Yep. Maybe mostly my favorite fleece bathrobe that I helped Fred select for me one

14

Christmas, now comfortably worn and wrap-around warm. He was certainly multi-layered.

As the fickle Covid threat expanded, we searched for toilet paper and paper towels like the rest of the country. Why did our collective social instincts demand that we stock up on toilet paper? This will forever be a mystery.

Fred reported on bare grocery store shelves and no traffic on the roadways. He once stopped for a squirrel as it casually sauntered, not leapt, across a four-lane highway, brazenly confident cars were no longer a danger.

Luckily, Fred and I had our roof and enough resources to get through this thing, so we were able to migrate between horror and amusement. There were jokes like, "They said a mask and gloves were enough to go to the grocery store, but they lied because everyone else had clothes on." And Internet anecdotes about how the buttons on people's jeans were social distancing as we collectively sat home and ate. Weekdays were renamed thisday, thatday, otherday, someday, yesterday, today, and nextday.

We had a few weeks of social distancing, hand-washing, double-masking, and privileged playfulness before Fred started feeling badly. His ability to smell went first. How odd. And then body aches with fever. I could see the flush beneath his wrinkly, long-tanned, skin. Progressively and most worrisome was his trouble breathing, likely exacerbated by his many years of being that tough-as-a-knot Marlboro man, living alone in his campus rez apartment smoking and championing his favorite hybrid maize. That is all I can say about that and even these words may not truly capture Fred's passions.

With him being ill, we knew to keep our distance, me upstairs, him down. We joked about how he was the older one —probably fought in the Peloponnesian Wars or something— so got to get sick first. We struggled not to give the virus the stature of tragedy; the feeling of brooding doom. I teased, "You always get to be the oldest." But my nudges were not funny.

What to do? I would put food on a tray for him, but we did not even know if it was safe for me to pick up his dishes after he ate, so little. How did this virus transfer? Air? Surface? Physical touch? Water-borne? What was its length of viability?

***

It was 3am when Fred touched my arm. I instinctively moved toward him, then remembered Covid, and backed away. He took hold of my hand and would not let go. His face looked terribly thin and suddenly now colorless, a tiny line between his brows where worry for the future seemed to rest. Hoarsely he whispered, "Trouble breathing."

One-handed, I called 911, wishing the numbers were closer together on the keypad. The EMTs came quickly, cloaked in their goggles and protective aqua garb. We all knew about pandemic-caused shortages in PPE, personal protective equipment. We had not all heard its crinkly vibe up close.

The Emergency Medical Technicians were kind, gentle, knowledgeable. So many people getting so very ill. They took Fred away in the ambulance and, of course, I could not go along, much less visit in the subsequent days. We were used to separations, but this was different. Our frightened loneliness felt thick.

As the ambulance pulled out of the driveway, I thought back to meeting Fred my freshman year in college.

I'd just graduated from a college-prep high school where we spent a year learning how to research and write our eventual Ph.D. dissertations; an assumption about what we would do in our collective futures. I was exploring the college library when Fred sidled up to me and introduced himself. He then offered to show me how the Dewey Decimal system worked.

It was sweet and I allowed him to explain how to find a given book. I'd never met anyone like him with his long hair and rural earthy ways. When we left the library, shoulders occasionally touching, he suggested that we sit under the massive oak near the library entrance. What oak? I'd not noticed its ancient beauty when I entered the building. But he had. We brought different eyes to our relationship that grew, like that tree, over time. Ah, Fred. My Fred.

He and I talked by hospital phone mornings, briefly. His breath was increasingly raspy and labored. Then his nurse told me they had put him on a ventilator and talked about how lucky we were to live where those machines were even available. The only sound on the phone calls the nurse orchestrated for us after that was the ventilator chirp. I did not know whether to have hope. The nurse promised to text a photo of Fred so I could see his progress. I guessed the news was not good, but no one could tell me how bad.

The photo was painful. Fred was being held, no, caressed, in the tender arms of a large African American man. His nurse. All I could see in the photo was Fred's ear and messy long gray hair. The nurse was double masked, wearing glasses and a face shield; covered, head to gloves, in PPE and wearing an identification tag showing his face to humanize him in spite of the gear. He held Fred like you would a sick and frightened child. Fetal position. Vulnerable. Less than.

I was not able to say goodbye to Fred. I will never know what his last moments were like. I didn't know the quality of the air he breathed. The kind nurse did. Time of death: 16:22.

Fred became a statistic, one of the millions who died.

We could not have a funeral or life celebration—distanced virtual funerals became the norm. Truth be told, Fred and I did not have family or local friends to invite to a funeral anyway. Living separately had pretty much ruled out events with other couples. Because we had no children, there was not a next generation to reminisce with. Our parents were gone. If people can be reclusive together, well then, we had been just that.

Fred's death hit me in waves, like water lapping in the soft spaces between gentle tides. I've heard it said that death is like ink being poured into water, not contracting but expanding. I hope that was true for Fred as I carried my sorrow in my bones. My mind wandered back to my father's dying, feeding him chocolate pudding that ignominiously dribbled onto his chin, when he was unable to feed himself, lying uncomfortably in that hospital bed. And then my mother's discomfited dying, angry at the dementia that was taking her too slowly. Her last coherent sentence was, "I never knew it would be so hard." Dying, that was.

I became aware that the younger woman I had once been was now gone forever. No living human would ever know who I had been. And there would never again be enough time to build the same depth of relationship I had had with Fred. I very simply did not have enough years of living left.

I remembered that Walt Whitman wrote something like, I am human and this is what happens to humans. Humans are aware of death.

* * *

Early on, Fred had playfully suggested I simply bury him in the backyard in a plain cardboard box. No fuss. But, with a Covid death, it was not immediately clear what special requirements might come into play for a person who died of infectious or communicable disease. So, I quit considering alternatives and simply had his body cremated. Fred's ashes were delivered to my doorstep in a hermetically sealed container. That felt so cold. So distant. So unbelievable. Someday I will spread his ashes on the rez (or on a hardware store parking lot – a place he had frequented -- as he and I had teased, if the pine box did not work out) and I'd eventually join him there. Wherever.

The space between is not so much.
I feel his presence.
I sense his touch.

I remembered that time, in India, when a family invited me to join them in the cremation of their father. It was a smoldering funeral pyre, open air, in a public park next to the lake where his ashes would eventually settle. Burning a body takes six hours. I had been, literally, just walking by. I stayed with them for an hour feeling the heat from the burning wood and the warmth of their invitation.

Loneliness and the need for touch is a hunger that many of us in the West do not even know we have.

But what next? What to do? I was all alone in the draft of loneliness. I couldn't even read; I couldn't focus.

ISOLATED LONELINESS

I wallowed, feeling sorrowful, somber, and isolated after Fred died. I felt ever older and even my sorrow seemed feeble. I did not want to be so alone. Nostalgia for what we had shared and regret for what we hadn't flooded my mind.

There was the material legacy of Fred's things. I kept sorting, organizing, collating, and stuffing things into smaller boxes. Detailed syllabi, student papers with red circled A's at the top right corner, gently scanned faculty memos; the stuff of teaching. And what about the turquoise-and-silver Native American belts he had worn. His brown felt hat, worn smooth. They were so him. Do you imagine that people transform into things after death? Could Fred's essence have conflated with a belt? Or a knot of pine? If he became pine, does that knot represent "love" for me? Could he live within the trees?

Do I try to make it through the rest of my life alone? Do I cry and grieve every day? Or do I get some gumption and reach out to others, even in Covid times?

Determined, I pulled myself up and explained to me that I only had a few years left on this earth, in my present recognizable form. I was healthy enough and needed to carry on with my own life in whatever ways I could. I was, after all, a human being.

Although I was unable to consciously articulate the thought, I wanted to be around people who were in pain and who understood loss. So, we could talk. They could understand, perhaps.

Come here; hold this sorrow with me. Share our grief.

It became increasingly obvious to me that I had no one. Yes, I owned a house. And yes, I had a wish to be able to smile during each twenty-four hours.

But do what? Deliver food to people's doorsteps? Such limited opportunities to help others during this pandemic. Should I rescue a cat? Should I name her Nala? Should I name him Rufus? But who would care for her or him when I went toes up?

The Internet became my virtual friend; a way to reach out to someone. Another human. It was a way to smile at little things like another olding and isolated woman who wrote, "It is good to have someone call on me daily, concerned about my car warranty."

And then I saw this shared online Facebook posting:

> **Please help! We Have a Young Woman in need of Temporary Shelter:**
> We have applied for all available shelter options, however everyone has waitlists. Hopefully we will have a better answer in a few days. I'd like to help her with shelter this week while we work on a plan going forward. We don't believe anyone should have to sleep outside in the elements. We believe in community support and know together we can make a difference!
> Every donation helps whether it's $5, $10, $20 or more....we do all we can to help.
> Please consider helping this woman by sharing our post or by donating; contact Eleanor

TEMPORARY

Key words and phrases stood out for me reading this call for help. "Temporary." "This week." "Outside in the elements."

Unfortunately—I hate it that I feel I must be wary all the time—my first thought was, *Is this a legitimate request?* The shelter is local and they do have a reasonable website promoting their good works. Their words are soothing and reassuring. *Is that enough information to make a determination of authenticity?* Scammers are very sophisticated these days. *But what's to scam on this?*

Okay, the young woman (*Does "young" mean 13 or 35?*) is in need of a temporary place to live, which tells me she doesn't have one right now. Where has she been living? With whom? Has she recently been tested for Covid and were the results negative? Obviously. Outside-in-the-elements implies she either is, or will be, homeless. That is unacceptable for anyone in this climate, and I do have this small but sturdy roof I could share, with more than enough food for two.

She is poor. Temporarily? Longer term? Does that suggest she will steal from me? Well, let's consider the things I have. Nearly all lie at the midpoint on a continuum between run-down/frayed and antique. The furniture and electronics have very little economic value, only sentimental connections. They are what Fred and I called "Early Parent" back in the day, leftovers from Fred's and my parents' homes. I suppose some would fall into the realm of antique but only because they were passed down through the generations. Still, they are shabby. And the electronics, well, imagine a tape deck and left-over floppy disks if you want to know how far out of synch I mostly am in that regard. Still, like my aged body, these things do work well enough. I was forced to purchase a flat screen TV when my local stations threatened to become inaccessible to my old TV. Best Buy set up the 19-inch LED for me. The one exception is the computer, which is state-of-the-art—my former teaching thingamajig, and access to the outside world.

I don't know how long the ad has been in place, so perhaps I can just respond and be thanked for my good intentions but learn that the young woman has been placed in a secure space. I could then get the virtuous credit without having to actually do anything. Maybe I could just send them $100 and be done. Keep my hands clean.

I could then return to my consideration of adopting a mature cat as company.

Even if she (the girl, not the cat) moves in, there is that word *temporary*. I can do most anything provisionally.

What would Fred have said? He would not want me to be alone all the time. He would weigh the pros and cons—with special emphasis on the pros—then likely conclude, "Go for it."

Okay, Fred, I will call Eleanor.

CASE FILE 381
ELEANOR'S CASE NOTES

Ruby Smith. Age 17. Pregnant, about five months she thinks, give or take. Recently homeless; the people she was staying with disappeared with their (and her) government Covid stimulus money leaving her with the clothes on her back and wrapped in that blue blanket. Months of back rent due. Six people living in the two-bedroom apartment that I wouldn't send a cockroach to, plus Ruby sleeping on the couch. Good news, her name wasn't on the lease. She is somewhere on that dividing line between adolescence and womanhood.

Her boyfriend is in the county jail after trying to steal money to get them by. She is tough, but shivering. She told me that life is trying to grind her down and has been for as long as she has had life. She is street-smart, a survivor, and actually seems pretty wise. But right now, it is a withering wisdom, not the kind that keeps a person on course day to day. All I had to offer her were stale cookies from the break room. She inhaled them, then asked if we had any olives.

We cannot let her stay on the streets. We have no available rooms and neither does anyone else right now. She will stay with me for tonight, even though this damn sure is a total rule violation (*don't record this*), especially since she could well be positive for Covid-19 given her exposed lifestyle.

I'm putting out a plea on Facebook. Maybe one of our supporters will step up for a few days, like fostering a kitten or helping a bird beating its wings against whatever is caging it.

Damn. They just keep coming. People in need.

Having to prove their lives have any value is such a constant cycle of stress from poverty and trauma and racism. It's definitely impacting mental health—theirs and maybe mine as well (*don't record this either*). They don't feel safe going to the doctor and scared to call the cops. Luckily Ruby came to me.

The whole system is deep-seated neglect. It's not going change of its own accord. I want to dedicate every penny we have to equity—women's health and racial equity, trans healthcare, prison healthcare—I want everyone who has experienced abuses to be served. Healthcare should be a right, not a privilege. If that means dismantling the whole damn system of care and designing something that actually serves everyone, then that's what I want to do. I see that now. Covid has taught us. Taught me.—Eleanor

* * *

Oh, my God. Another skinny white lady. Nose up.
Thinks she knows about my experiences but has no clue.
At least she will find us somewhere to stay.

"Thanks for the soda and cookies, Eleanor. My gut feels way better. My baby must of liked it too; she sleepin' now."

"How do you know it's a girl?" Eleanor asks the question, rhetorically, while focusing most of her attention on typing case notes.

"Well, I haven't been tested, but I want a girl."

"Okay, listen, Ruby. That request for housing that I put on Facebook came back with a response already. One hour! A record. The shelter doesn't know this woman named Zoe, but she sounds good. Her husband died of Covid so she is aware of the need for masking and social distancing while you are staying with her until we get your Covid test results back. You will both be safe."

Shaking her head in a slow circle, Ruby Blue sucks her teeth. "Wait, wait. She's White? And she's old? Hold up a sec. I don't do White people. And I don't do old. I ain't scared, I just think not."

"Honey, we don't have any alternatives now and it is just for the short term, until we can get you into a shelter."

"This is becoming a sad situation. All I feel is alone, well, me and my baby."

"Look, don't let your mouth get your head in trouble. I've counseled many girls in your situation and things are going to be okay. This is just a rough patch," Eleanor says as she reaches in with a one-finger tap on Ruby Blue's shoulder, violating social distancing regs, but wanting to offer some compassionate consolation to this frightened and very alone young woman.

"Listen. I ain't meanin' nothing by it, I'm just askin', no, just sayin'. But a person gets herself in a tight spot, there ain't much she can do. It ain't up to her no longer. Guess I haven't got many choices. I'll have to see how other people are forced to live," Ruby Blue says with a little sideways half-smile. Whispering to herself, *Can't never give up. Things will get better.* She narrows her eyes reflectively as she pulls the stained blue blanket more tightly around her shoulders. A half-shiver.

"We have called an Uber to take you to Zoe's house. Just wait out front. I wish the best of luck to you. I'll be back in touch as soon as I find you a place in one of the shelters. Remember, this is just temporary. Choices aren't always between what's right and what's wrong, but between what's right and what's best. Here are a few maternity clothes to take with you. Sorry we don't have a suitcase, but this black bag will have to work for now."

"Yes, ma'am," Ruby Blue stammers. "Thanks...until we meet again."

* * *

The steps outside Eleanor's office are uneven and chipped as Ruby Blue maneuvers clumsily into a sitting position, avoiding the wet spaces, and scrunching the top of the black bag, then letting it rest beside her. Ruby Blue ponders.

> *Sun's warm on my back, waitin' for the Uber. Snowbanks are wet on the edges, melting for a minute. Beneath the melt, light-colored alley dust is showin'. Glad I got this blanket and Marcus' hoodie; why they leave me without even a coat. Don't they know I'm prego; even have that prego brain, all unorganized, sloppy like an unmade bed. Maybe that's why they left me.*

> *Look at all these wet kids racing around. No school. Don't know whether I'd have loved or hated that when I was a child. I did like school and free lunch. Does this*

shelter even have WiFi? Do these kids have laptops?
Does anyone care? Kids' face coverings at half mask,
their mouths covered but not their noses. One kid has
his mask over his eyes. Pointless. But they are kids and
maybe don't get Covid. That mom is calling her kid a
piece of shit. I wonder what kind of mom I will be; what
kind of parents Marcus and I will be? We 'bout to be
givin' our baby girl a lot of love.

First thing I'm gonna do at this Zoe person's house is
take a bath. I smell like outside.

OLD. WHITE.

As the Uber pulls up in front of the house, Zoe opens the door.

"Hello. Come in. My name is Zoe Smyth and you will be staying with me just for a day, maybe two."

"I'm Ruby." The words come out more ragged than intended as she twists through the doorway, a firm grip on the garbage bag with one hand and the blue blanket with the other; arriving with empty pockets and tempered hope.

Her name Smith?

"Just put your things here on the chair."

Ruby Blue sluffs off the blanket and lets it and the bag drop on the old-fashioned chair, wooden arms and legs with animal feet carved on them, and shiny, formal-looking striped fabric, like you might see in a fancy hotel lobby. "Thanks."

> *This place smells stale, like ol' books and Pine-Sol. She's White like Casper and wrinkly like clothes fresh out of the dryer. Damn, and why is she already tryin' to get rid of me? But, it's not about just me anymore. Gotta do this for the baby. Remember, it's only temporary.*

Zoe gasps inwardly.

> *This girl is looking at me with unreadable eyes that won't meet mine, yet won't look away from my face. OH MY GOD. She is pregnant! And tattoos! This isn't going to happen. She can't possibly stay here. Her eyes are*

dull. She doesn't blink. Her head is lowered like an animal about to charge. There is something wrong with her. Covid? No smile lines around her eyes, but I guess she is only 17 so they might not be there yet. So young. SO pregnant! No, I will call Eleanor right now and tell her to send the Uber back. This cannot happen.

"Would...would you like something to drink?" Zoe stammers.

"Yes, do you have soda? It settles my stomach."

Oh, my God, this girl IS sick. Her face is like the drawing of the lion's face on, what's the name of that book by D'Egville? Into the Lion's Den. *That's it, Brits going to South Africa. The arrogant, but frightened stare of those lion eyes. Dangerous eyes. Unblinking eyes. African eyes. She is BLACK too. BLACK and pregnant. BLACK and tattooed. BLACK and pierced. What have I gotten myself into?*

"I have some green tea. Want to try that?" Zoe offers, moving into formal, "gracious hostess" mode.

"Sure. Yo, where's your bathroom at?"

"Right down the hall," Zoe gestures to her left.

As the electric kettle begins to heat the tea water, Zoe picks up the phone. Eleanor answers. Half-whispering, Zoe pleads, "Eleanor, you need to send the Uber back. This isn't going to work. She is pregnant! You didn't tell me that."

"Well, we don't have any options right now. It's just for a night or two. She isn't about to deliver, so you won't have to deal with breaking water and the like."

"No. No. Seriously. Send the Uber back."

"It is just for a night or two. I'll call as soon as I locate a shelter bed somewhere in the city. I'm looking."

Big hesitation, then Zoe sighs, "Well. Okay, okay. I guess."

Overhearing part of the conversation, Ruby Blue rolls her eyes. "My pregnancy won't rub off on ya. It's not contagious. I'm not a thief. I won't steal your precious China plates. I do have manners, thank you very much."

Pretending she didn't hear the China comment, Zoe utters, "There is green tea and black tea. Which do you prefer."

"Don't matter."

It really don't matter. I ain't drinking this shit anyway.

"I guess you should stay out of the kitchen while we drink our tea, unmasked. I'll just put your cup on this folding table. My Fred and I used this as a way to pass food when he was so sick, to avoid having contact."

Shaken, Ruby Blue blurts out, "Wait a minute. Your husband died in this house?! I ain't stayin' here!" Ruby Blue twists toward her blanket and the black bag, ready to run.

"No, no, Ruby. It was a month ago and he died in the hospital, with a nurse gently holding his head."

"Oh, sorry. I can't get sick, with the baby and all. I do my best, I really do."

Water gurgles in the teapot and Zoe offers, "I made green tea for you. It will be soothing for, uh, you and the baby. It's herbal."

"I've never had green tea before, or any tea actually," Ruby Blue utters, voice low with an accompanying scowl.

The two women sit, distanced, unmasked for the first time, looking at each other, slowly. Visually circling like lionesses around a carcass. Wary. Awkward. Intense.

Oh, God, and a nose piercing. A knife! Are there more tattoos I can't see? She isn't like my students were. One night. Only one night. I won't sleep for a minute.

Ruby Blue sips the hot tea and frowns, "Got any sugar?"

"Sure." Zoe places an antique sugar bowl painted with tiny pink roses and a small silver spoon on the folding table that separates the women. A hand-embroidered tablecloth decorated with cross-stitched daisies and dandelions, marred by two small amoeba-shaped stains that never came out in washings, covers the worn card table.

I've never seen a Black hand touch the sugar bowl. What would Granny have said about this image?

In her teacher voice, Zoe suggests, "Not too much, girl. You need to stay healthy for the baby."

"Don't be calling me 'girl.' I'm a woman," Ruby Blue replies sullenly.

What, you my mama or somethin'? No, more like the age of an OG.

Uncomfortable, Zoe changes the subject. "Want to go for a walk after we finish our tea?"

"I don't do walks in the cold; my ankles swolle' anyways," Ruby Blue replies, half turning away and avoiding eye contact.

"Well, that is a reason to walk; motion is lotion."

What am I, her keeper, her mother? I sound like my own long-deceased mom. Drat. What is she really thinking, being in this space, my space?

"What?" Half listening as she looks around the living room that has a definite museum feel to it, Ruby Blue twists her head to the side in a questioning motion.

"Keep those joints moving. This is what my Qigong teacher always instructs as she implores us, her senior students, to work on flowing movement, gentle breathing, and, yes, mindfulness. Well, before Covid that was."

"Joints? Qigong?"

What the hell is this woman talkin' about? Movin' joints?

Seeing Ruby Blue's perplexed look, Zoe adds, "You know, knees, ankles, toes."

With pure disbelief, Ruby Blue pauses, then mutters, "Ohhhhh, those kinda joints."

"What does your doctor say about your swollen ankles?"

How do I talk with this angry young woman? She truly is not like my students were. I'd say deferential is the word I'd use to describe my student/professor relationships. Is this question too personal? She is clearly five or six months pregnant. Oh, God.

"I ain't have no doctor and I'm not figuring to see one in a hurry. That costs money and I sure wouldn't be in this mess if I had any of that."

Who does this lady think she is? Read the room. Why is she all in my business? She don't need to worry about me. I got me.

"No doctor? Have you had any pre-natal checkups?"

What if she is ill? She looks healthy enough, if sullen and sad, other than those ankles which, yes, are swollen. Depressed? Likely she is depressed; weighted down mentally and physically. A spirit of heaviness. That makes sense. I can connect with that feeling. I'm smiling inside remembering I was just telling myself, after Fred's death, that I wanted to be around people who were in pain and who understood loss. So, we could talk, hold sorrow together, and share our exhausting grief. Maybe that wish has been granted in an odd way.

"I said, I ain't got a doctor. This ain't none of your business anyway. Stay in your lane. You don't even know me like that."

Who drinks this stuff? There ain't enough sugar on the planet to make tea drinkable.

Hesitantly, because Ruby Blue appears visibly angry,

I'll allow my mother to channel again.

"Well, I think you will need to fix that. Hey, you could even find out the gender of your baby at a doctor visit. Do you want a boy?"

Angrily, "I don't want no boy."

"Why?" Zoe visualizes.

There is that scene from Lion King where Rafiki holds up Simba, the son, with such pride for all the animal kingdom to see and admire. A boy! A male child! The next king!

Exasperated, Ruby Blue explains, "When my cousin had one of those gender reveal parties, she found out she was having a girl and her dad went into the garage and cried."

"Cried?" Zoe tips her head sideways, eyes squinting. Trying to understand.

"Yes, cried with relief because the world ain't safe for Black boys. They either end up dead or in prison. And everyone was wanting the baby girl who would look like her daddy because that's good luck."

"Ah," Zoe sips from the thin-lipped teacup and nods her head back, with feigned interest.

Speaking her truth, Ruby Blue pleads, "Look, I really just want to take a shower and lie up in bed. That cool with you?"

Can a person feel violently unshowered? I think so.

"Sure."

> *There is no way this is going to work out for more than one night. We come from different worlds. We don't speak the same language. She didn't even know what a joint is.*

"Let's take your things to the bedroom, down the hall on the right."

"This is all I have." Ruby Blue picks up the black garbage bag from the chair that Zoe had inherited from her grandmother. A sparkly stiletto heel has pierced through the bottom of the bag. Both women look down at the shoe.

Defensively, "This shoe ain't mine. Must have been in the bag Eleanor gave me."

Eyes averted and ignoring what she perceives to be an excuse, Zoe nods.

> *Why does she need sparkly high heels in her condition? Is that connected to how she got pregnant? One night. One night. One night, I can do this.*

"There is soap and shampoo in the tub, Ruby."

"Thanks."

Ruby Blue shuts the door behind her, thinking quietly to herself,

> *What am I suppose' to do with these White-girl products? And, what have I done? They gone. Marcus locked up. No room at the shelter and this Zoe Smith woman. Is she thinking that shoe is mine? Do I look like a stiletto kinda girl? How on GOD's green earth would I even fit into it?*

Zoe walks back down the hall.

> *What have I done? Tattooed. Pierced. A pregnant teenager in my house! It's only one night.*

But, then, returning to Ruby Blue's bedroom with fresh towels, Zoe overhears giggling on the phone. "She's so old her memory in black and white." Laughter. "But I'm not scared by no one, especially a White woman."

Then, "That don't make no sense, but don't have to. She White. That's the way the cracker crumbles."

Zoe knocks on the door. Ruby Blue sheepishly opens it, realizing her words might have been overheard.

Damn, now I feel bad. Maybe I shouldn't have said that.

Eyes downcast, Zoe hands in the towels and backs away.

Ruby Blue awkwardly looks down, mumbling, "Oh, my bad."

RUBY BLUE

RUBY BLUE

People call me Ruby. But allow me to reintroduce myself. My name is Ruby Blue.

That's me.

I speak as I am. Tell them. Color doesn't define me; color is political, not human. My nappy hair? Proud of my locks. Can't nobody tell me how to live. I got a nose like my daddy's was, which you might call an acquired taste. Sure, I wear a knife nose ring (a good childbirth vibe to cut the pain) and tell the world I'm a survivor, but I'm not one of those whose mouth's full of violence. I speak my truth. I ain't one to play with.

I know the power of their language, and I know how to switch it up. At times I be like, "That's not unusual." But then I'm like, "It be like that sometimes." Bi-lingual. A code switcher who can toggle between standard and street.

Street talk is sound and rhythm. Pulse and beat. Spoken word. Dance and expression. All of this is part of the message; way more than the mere dropping of s's from plurals and suffixes from past-tense verbs. I know what a past participle is. I ain't stupid; I can speak their language real well. If I choose to. Did you ever think about how we have only had two generations when my people could read and study without slavery laws against readin' and writin' and without segregation limits?

And if they see me as deficient, expressing sympathy, even hatred, for me and my perceived ineptitude, well, that's on them. Prejudice. They lookin' at what I don't have or who I am not. Born deficient and doomed to servitude 'til my grave, in their eyes. Not one who will make it out. Less than. In their eyes. Their words, not mine.

Since when was making them comfy my job? Why should they be at ease? It ain't my job to educate 'em on race or equality.

Sometimes I choose to be invisible and walk softly, quiet my voice so as not to awaken those who be sleepin'. The streets taught me I'm supposed to keep my head down, my mouth shut, and get home before the sun goes down and the streetlights come on. I'm supposed to know my place. Take up space only when necessary.

I have walked onto polished floors where they assumed I wanted the food pantry in the basement rather than the law firm on the top floor. I've graciously given random directions when they think I'm an employee rather than a customer like them. Sometimes they wait to take the next elevator. Sometimes I hear doors lock as I walk by. Some will speak to me in loud tones. Slowly. They don't call it a clutch for no reason as women pull their Louis Vuitton bags to their breasts when I approach. Don't nobody want yo shit, lady!

Even on something as public as a bus, no White people sit next to me; don't touch.

They are caught up in the trapdoor of their own self-reference. No matter how degraded their lives, they still believe they possess the right genetics, the correct bloodlines, and pale superiority. No matter what evil befalls them, they still never have to fear reaching into, what they perceive as, the gutter of blackness. If given the choice between equality for all (democracy) or whiteness, how many would choose whiteness?

Sometimes the grind folds back on itself, twisting time, and the past and the present collapse into each other. Then that voice in my head goes, *Don't throw up your hands, roll up your sleeves. No one carries weight like a Black woman. A strong Black woman.*

I swag, strut to the mirror. "Wassup?" I say louder, "Wassup, girl? You homeless! Broke and pregs? As pregnant as it gets. Watcha gonna do? What are we gonna do to get me and my baby out of this mess?" Then I'm thinkin' I'll never be able to protect you, my baby, like I am right now, so be safe and grow strong. I ain't letting this get me down, even if I am goin' be mothering on the margins of society. Like Tupac offered, *Keep your head up; we keep'n this or let'n it go*? We keep'n. Can't wait to meet you when the time comes, my baby girl. What would I name you? What would Daddy name you? What kind of little shoes will I get you? Some Js? Some Air Force 1s? Okay, enough of this rant.

I'm Ruby Blue Smith. If you cannot pronounce my name correctly, then just call me Ms. Smith.

NOW WHAT?

Moving back into hostess mode, Zoe mulls.

Now what? Dinner next? Someone to cook for besides only me. What do I have that's good for the baby and mom? Spinach salad with strawberries.

Chicken breast with wild rice. Green beans and carrots. A cookie for dessert – those molasses cookies are in the freezer. Maybe peppermint tea this time since the green wasn't a big hit. Surely the smell of the chicken cooking will bring her out of the bedroom.

I'll just try to read while it cooks. If I had a sleepy cat, it would curl up with me now in the late afternoon sun. A nice cat would be so much easier than a prickly human. Maybe I'll go to the Humane Society after the Uber picks up Ruby tomorrow. Well, if I can get in. I suppose cat adoptions are happening online now. The world is so broken. Dysfunctional. Evil Covid. But I cannot overthink this.

Zoe naps, Faulkner's *The Sound and The Fury*—the story of downfall to renewal—open on her lap.

* * *

"Knock, knock, Ruby. I've got some good food for you and the baby. Come to dinner." Zoe walks back to the kitchen.

Chagrinned, Ruby Blue mumbles as she is walking down the hall, "Okay. Finally. I'm hungry as hell!"

As Ruby Blue sits, she blurts out, "Can we just hit reset? Let the shit go and move forward? That cool with you?"

With a sudden and surprising flash of warmth toward this young woman, Zoe smiling and teasing, imitates, "Yeah, we cool. Enjoy and fill your belly."

Now there are two folding tables between the kitchen and living room piled with plates, silverware, classic flowered linen napkins, and steaming food, except the cookies, of course. Ruby Blue mounds her plate with chicken, rice, and snippets of spinach. She eats hungrily, mightily. The social distancing is good because the women can have their own space and not feel like polite conversation is needed immediately.

Resting her fork for a second, Ruby Blue requests, "I never could do silence. Mind playing some music? It's how you understand life. Spiritual meditations, gospel, blues, jazz, and then R & B, rock n' roll, hip hop, or rap. All of it speaks to me. It raises the big questions and allows space for self-reflection."

"Okay. Is jazz good for dinner? Or "Love Me Tender" by Elvis, which has always been a truly great love song?" Zoe smiles mischievously, knowing that this isn't the song or artist Ruby Blue would choose.

Ruby Blue misses the tease, not expecting playfulness. Politely, she suggests, "Or a little Aretha?"

"I have a Ray Charles album. *Georgia on my Mind?* Good dinner music. That okay?"

Ruby Blue nods. "Hit the Road Jack" begins to play, and after momentary discomfort passes across Ruby Blue's eyes, with Zoe remembering that Ruby had recently been abandoned, they first snicker and then laugh together, although somewhat awkwardly. Still, it is a shared moment.

We might talk later about that desertion, or not, because she is leaving tomorrow. Who knows. But for now, something lighter. I do know how to talk with young people; well, with college students anyway. In my teaching, I had practice. Mostly women, though, and nearly all White.

"If you had been cooking our dinner, Ruby, what would you have made for us?"

Hesitating, then smiling and remembering somewhere, sometime past, Ruby Blue speaks, with the second smile the women have shared. "First of all. There would be a lotta soda, 'cause I get none of that around here!" Looking at Zoe with a smirk, "I'm just teasin'."

"I could really go for some red beans and rice, with a fried pork chop. Then some Wonder Bread, you know, to soak up all them juices. All this talk makes me think of Granny's baked mac-n-cheese. I remember thinking it was so good, she must've put her foot in it. That woman could split a nickel six ways with the neighbor kids coming 'round."

Ruby Blue looks up, pondering.

Memories. What good people. Where have they all gone?

"Probably not this kind of chicken, though. Maybe some chicken livers. Sometimes a country biscuit with molasses. And other times, mustard greens, I like greens more than this raw spinach o' yours. No worries though. My least favorite was chitlins, but they were saved by the black-eyed peas.

"One of my favorite treats is a yam with a spoonful of melted butter poured over top. Watch that butter seep in, sweet and hot.

"And, don't get me started on the smells. The good. The ways cabbage or sweet potato pie smells up the house. Or the bad that leaves an oil scent in the house so you have to boil Fabuloso to get rid of the smells."

Ain't nothin' better than soul food.

Zoe sees Ruby's eyes glisten, visible even from the distance. Grief? Sadness? Homesickness? Longing? For what? Who? Grandparents? Aunts? She doesn't ask, but thinks:

Eternally there has been the connection between food and love. Maybe that is what Ruby is feeling right now. Remembering right now.

Ray Charles begins singing, "*I can't stop loving you,*" and Zoe watches Ruby's eyes gleam even more. "*Those happy hours…*"

"Are you thinking about the father of your child," Zoe asks quietly, carefully, thinking about losing Fred and how much her life has changed in just a few weeks.

"Yes, of course. My baby-daddy is in jail right now. He tried to get us some money before the stimulus cards came, but then got caught up."

After a pause, "Would you like a molasses cookie?"

That is what my mother would have done to change the subject from something uncomfortable or awkward. I truly need to stop being my mother.

Ruby Blue nods, "Sure. Molasses cookies remind me of my childhood, back in the day. When I was a shorty in elementary school, we used to get those as a snack all the time. Frosted. I remember eating too many, getting sick to my stomach, and then instantly regretting my decision—which might be why I don't eat them as often now. You mind if I take the cookie to bed with me?"

Zoe can see tears continuing to glisten in Ruby's eyes as she hands the young woman a plate, the cookie resting on a small napkin.

Respecting her space, Zoe turns away, saying, "Sure, please just leave your dishes on the folding table. G'night, Ruby."

* * *

Ruby Blue shuffles to the bathroom twice during the night.

> *Good thing there was that nightlight I put in for Fred. Yep, Ruby is pregnant, and that baby is pushing on her bladder after all the peppermint tea that she did like better than the green tea. Fred, drawing on his deep-rooted connection with Native American life and ways, used to say that women have a natural bond with water, being life-bearers who carry babies in internal ponds and then birth them in a wave. What is more feminine than water?*

> *Lots of bathroom trips are normal. Does Ruby have any idea what to expect in the coming months? Has she talked with women who have given birth? Well, this won't be my problem; but women do protect each other around what delivery and birthing entails. And she hasn't even seen a doctor, already in her third trimester. I'll tell her case worker, Eleanor, to make sure she sees a doctor soon.*

* * *

"Well, good morning, Ruby. No call yet from the shelter, but I'll let you know. I see you have put on some of the new maternity clothes they sent along with you. I don't see the glitzy high heel!"

Seeing Ruby startle, Zoe tries to reassure her, "It was just a joke."

Sleepily and defensively, Ruby Blue thinks,

> *Sometimes who you are perceived to be, comes down to the smallest things.*

"Those were already in the bag when she gave it to me; they ain't mine. You got any coffee?"

"Sure. You must have needed that sleep," Zoe attempts to make polite conversation.

"Yeah, I feel safe to sleep here." Ruby Blue glances around at the tired furniture in the orderly, dirt-free living room.

"I'm glad you feel safe. Since it looks like you might be staying for another day, what food would you like me to order from the grocery store? They deliver in the afternoons."

In a testy voice, "Can we talk about that in a minute? I just need coffee. You like a morning person or somethin'? Damn, I just need a moment to wake up."

Zoe, facetiously, "I guess that is true, if we consider 11:30 to be morning!"

"Okay, okay. I expect you'd be less of a morning person if you had a bag of snakes kicking inside your stomach all the time! You got any kids?"

Turning her head toward the sink, Zoe mutters, "I was pregnant once," then changes the subject, "So, I like that maternity top you have on. Interesting that they created it with stripes going around your body. Bold. It shows off your baby bump. Do they still talk about baby bumps?"

"Look, can I just have some coffee? Please!" Ruby Blue begs.

> *Does this woman ever stop talking? Silence. I just want silence. People who live alone seem to talk more than anyone. They just do. Got stuff stored up to say and no one to listen, so they gotta get it all out when somebody else is around. On the far end of lonely, I suppose. Probably like me too if I'm being honest.*

"Yes. Sorry."

Ruby Blue sips her coffee, now that it is finally quiet. No music playing now. Noiseless.

Zoe putters around the sink, rearranging dishes and pretending to do something important.

* * *

A bit later, "I'm woke, now. The colors in this top good and it's warm, temperature-wise, I mean. I think bright colors look vulgar against my dark skin. They make me stand out too much, and too many clothes are not cut for my skinny shape. When I'm not pregnant, I mean. Now they are good, these shelter clothes are pretty good, for used. I was never big in fashion but also did not want White people to see me in like cheap, Goodwill clothes, like some poverty-stricken outcast, who is off the chain or cuttin' a fool in jeans with bad holes.

"White kids can dress that way, but I never went far from the crib in sweats and sneakers, mostly because it ain't safe to have that look anywhere beyond my hood. I would dress to gain respect. At the end of the day, it's important to the Black culture. I think my restrained fashion vibe was what drew Marcus to me. He knows how to treat a woman. He's my man."

> *What would my great-auntie be thinking of me now, looking like this in used maternity clothes? I remember the time she dressed me for church, all in pink. Even my shoes and socks were pink, walking on that broken asbestos-tiled basement floor, with the bright colored bulletin boards; Jesus' picture on the walls always asking WWJD. And the smell of fish frying and grits boiling in chicken broth.*

"I'm rememberin' my great-auntie always wore a fresh flower and an elaborate hat for church, with feathers and shit. Dark stockings. That was her thing. She looked extra."

"Ruby! This feels like more words than you have said in 20 hours total. We have got to come back to lots of these points later on. Want more coffee?"

"Ain't no thing. I only go out—well, before I was homeless—dressed up real nice, with my hair braided neat, and my face lookin' right. Yes, can I have more coffee? And that looks like toast or something over there. I'm so hungry."

"How about if we move straight to lunch? Do you like grilled cheese sandwiches with tomatoes?"

"Sure. Two or three, even."

* * *

After lunch, as Ruby Blue returns to her room to take a nap, Zoe silently wonders about her guest.

How long has it been since she had a safe and warm place to sleep and enough food to eat? What does she see when she looks at me. What does she think?

Eleanor calls from the shelter around 1:30. They have no bed for Ruby to move to that night and even if they did find something, single women (without children) are usually housed in the shelters with men. Tough. That just isn't a good option for Ruby, being pregnant and all.

"Could she just stay a while longer?" Eleanor requests.

"Of course, she can," Zoe accepts.

SWEET POTATO

Zoe hangs up the phone and thinks, again, about food.

Since she is staying another day, I'll quickly order some sweet potatoes to add to the grocery store delivery this afternoon to make that sweet potato waffle recipe I found (while looking up sweet potato pie). I have the cinnamon and nutmeg. Just need some sour cream and pecans, if they have them at the store. So many things are not available now. Bare shelves, I hear. Sounds straight forward. Won't Ruby be pleased with this surprise dinner. Oh, and syrup too. Need that. And some stomach-soothing soda for her.

* * *

Rubbing her eyes, Ruby Blue walks down the hallway toward the living room, noticing the setting sun reflecting golden on the far kitchen wall. Groceries had been left on the front steps, and Zoe washes the produce, now a familiar part of her Covid-prevention routine. With permission, Ruby Blue pulls the old-fashioned velvet striped chair to the kitchen doorway where she can be more comfortable to talk with, and watch Zoe in the kitchen.

"I'd love me some coffee."

A hot cup of coffee is placed on the folding table and Ruby Blue wraps her hands around it, siphoning its comforting warmth.

After a few minutes of silence as Zoe stirs pecans into the mashed sweet potatoes, Ruby Blue volunteers, "I don't normally do old people. But as I see your hands stirring the batter for those sweet potato waffles, just for me, I am thinking of a song I always loved. Heard it in church sometimes. Bill Witters? Withers? Not sure—wrote the song about his grandmother; a slave. He recently died, during Covid.

"His grandmother had those hands, like your hands, I imagine. Well, Black hands and kind of, what, well, used. Hands that have touched and worked and loved. In the song, Withers sings 'bout how Granny's hands can sooth an unwed mother, lift her face and say she understands that woman really loves that man. Granny remembers what that kind of love feels like. Put yo'self in Jesus' hands. In Granny's hands, he sings. Maybe those hands recognize the dignity and worth of all of God's children. I was jus' thinkin' about that. You are old but you are nice."

"Thanks, Ruby. That's high praise. And now if these waffles are any good, we are making progress. More good sleep coming for you and your baby too."

A few minutes of silence pass, then Ruby Blue tilts her head asking, "What happened to yo' baby, you being pregnant?"

"Let's talk about that another time," Zoe defers.

"You know, that is such a White person thing to do. Y'all never wanna go beneath the surface; never wanna talk about anything. Anything that could be a source of conflict like race or religion or color or life or even humanity, at the table, or anywhere. Ignore the important stuff. Don't deal with shit. Is that you? We outta the small talk. Now we got nowhere to go.

Be all color-blind or whatever? See, this is why I always be stank around White women."

Zoe stops stirring, turns, and looks squarely at Ruby, reflecting on the importance of their initial attempt at a deeper conversation. "First, we cannot generalize to all White people. That is prejudice—pre-judging—and not something you would let me do to you, right?"

Ruby Blue slowly shakes her head.

Geeze. Now we tryin' to pull the White fragility card? Already!

"You don't think I know about prejudice? You know from books. I know from bein' in the streets."

Zoe turns toward the bowl and stirs with more vigor, thinking,

What's this girl up to? Just when I was thinking we were getting past some of the awkwardness, she comes in my face about me being pregnant which, damn it, is none of her business. I should never have said anything. That was 1000 years ago. How do I respond to these comments? Why are so many Black people so aggressive and angry? Hum, is that a statement of prejudice too?

Ignoring the remark on book-learning versus experience on the streets (which hints at an uncomfortable truth), Zoe states, "Okay, I'll violate my own rule and generalize anyway. Many White women, I believe, are the peacekeepers in relationships or even business situations. You know, friendly, empathetic, and respectful. Always smoothing things over. Do you agree, Ruby?"

Pursing her lips and shaking her head back and forth, Ruby Blue hisses and rolls her eyes, "Nah, I don't believe in that shit. It's the exact opposite."

Every time I try talkin' with White people it's like this! They always thinking they some kind of savior. What's with them? Peacekeepers? Yeah. No! Not really. More like colonizers or predators preying on our Black kings. Or maybe just submissive; too scared to talk back. Are we through now?

Pouring batter into the waffle iron, then turning back toward Ruby, Zoe talks about an incident that happened while she was teaching.

"I was in a faculty meeting once—the entire faculty, maybe 100 people. It was the first gathering of the fall semester when we were all fresh from our summer of planning and reading and just being; eager to begin a new year of teaching and interactions. A newly hired African American woman took offense at something that was said—I don't remember what—and she lambasted the whole group. She was standing and screaming at us.

"We had been a campus team with lots of history and camaraderie and there she was, yelling. Yelling at another staff member, actually, but including everyone in the incident. It was enormously uncomfortable and, frankly, we were not used to having someone try to change the way we had always done things. She was let go very shortly after that. Sure, she might have had some points to make, but the approach was definitely a turn-off and a put-down for us. We did not learn anything from that other than to avoid this prickly woman at all costs.

"I never figured out why she was so angry; had such a chip on her shoulder. I think most of the faculty—at least I know this was true for me—would have liked to establish a relationship with her, have connections across the races. But I was afraid to even approach her after that incident. It felt to me like she was covered in shards of broken glass. So, no, no further connections occurred, although I did single out the White staff member who got the brunt of the yelling and told her I was sorry that had happened."

Ruby Blue cringes in disgust, unobserved by Zoe who is by now beating lumps out of the waffle batter, ignoring the caution written in the recipe: "Do not overmix the waffle batter; it should be a little bit lumpy."

Ruby Blue looks down at her hands gripped together on her lap, feeling the skin tighten over her knuckles, then rubs one hand over her distended pregnant belly, partly hidden by the flowered tablecloth. She feels exasperation gushing upward from the soles of her feet.

Does this White lady even hear herself right now? No wonder the new employee was yellin'—full of frustration—scared of change. Y'all wanna stay stuck in your ol' ways; too used to bein' comfortable, not even takin' time to be open-minded. Then y'all let her go!? For what? See this is some shit you people do that keeps us down. Wanna steal our ideas, but never wanna let us speak or express ourselves freely like y'all do.

Prickly!? Covered in broken glass!? Why? 'Cause she had a bad day!? A chip on her shoulder!? What, just like y'all, not trying to understand her point of view.

Afraid!? Why the fuck were you afraid!? If she was White, would you still have been so afraid? I bet you wouldn't even have flinched. Imagine being new, in a place where there weren't many Black workers and wanting to change something for the better, seeing the whole picture, but not given the time or space to be heard. What would you do?

You felt sorry for her? What a cop-out. White fragility at its finest.

And I can't even be honest with you and tell you what I'm thinkin'. You'd probably be afraid of me; probably think I'm just some crazy Black woman—all aggressive and angry.

Brow furrowed, Ruby Blue has a stern, yet sad, look on her face. She winces, turning toward Zoe, seeing her, and realizing there is no comprehension of the annoyance that is going through her mind.

What a shame. This White woman just ain't gettin' it.

But Granny's rule was, "You ass eat, you ass speak." Ruby Blue frowns. Then, as a way of quieting and moving beyond the unspoken judgments, she offers, "Uh, yo lopsided waffle smokin.' I never imagined no White woman comin' up with the most crooked food I've ever seen."

Ruby Blue smiles the way she knows she does when she thinks she has said something amusing. Something witty.

Fussing with the waffle iron that was not used to cooking vegetables, and the waffle that was, in fact, lopsided, Zoe smiles back, having no insight into what Ruby Blue has been thinking in the previous moments.

"Look, Ruby, we cannot force one another into talks about sensitive issues, like race, or pregnancy. It has to be mutual. How do we separate out the emotions? Should we? Maybe I'll talk about my pregnancy with you later on, if we have a 'later on' together, but this isn't a good time when the waffle is burning UP!"

> *How do I get out of this conversation right now? I'll change the topic to what I heard on the news this afternoon as the Black Lives Matter, the BLM protests—some say riots—expand across the country. That young Black woman being interviewed was saying she wouldn't go to the police for help, no matter what was going on. I have wondered about this. Police interactions across race. That's a good topic.*

As she digs the waffle off the hot iron in pieces and reaches across the card table, putting one waffle chunk on Ruby Blue's plate, Zoe asks, "But, okay, here is a question for you. If you were in trouble—like when you were homeless and your guy was in jail and your money was stolen—did you reach out to the police for help?"

Furrows deepen between Ruby Blue's eyes as she chews the piece of waffle. She shakes her head slightly and raises one hand, palm up, swallowing, questioning. Disbelieving.

Pointing her fork at Zoe, she says, "You funny as hell, ol' woman. Hell, nah! We talkin' about generations of lived experience that you don't understand. I'm gonna have to school you on some game for sure! If a police car were to pull up behind me, maaaaannnn, my heart beats outta my chest. Instant panic. Knowin' I did nothing wrong, but still can't catch my breath before the cop makes it to the window. Can't think straight. Nervous. To the cop, I'm actin' suspicious. But the reality is, I'm just worried about makin' one wrong movement that grants permission to shoot first and ask questions later."

Waiting for the waffle iron to get hot again, Ruby Blue asks,

"Can I tell you a story? One time, when I was out with some friends, past curfew, on our way home, and we got stopped. In reality, racially profiled, maybe because the cop was White. But anyway, at the time, my car window wouldn't roll down and I had to open the door. Instantly, I saw him reach for his holster and I frantically yelled, 'Woah, woah, woah, the window doesn't work. We are not going anywhere!!' He relaxed and asked us what we were doin' and where we were goin'. We responded that we were leaving from a friend's house and I was going to drop everyone off. One of my friends in the back said, 'It's really none of your business,' and that pissed the cop off and he made us get out of the car. Once he saw he was outnumbered, he called for back-up. I pleaded with him to let us go and that I was sorry for my friend's comment. After talking for a while, he finally let us go with a warning."

Zoe questions, "Do you really think you got racially profiled or was it because…"

Ruby Blue interrupts and changes the subject, "I'm hungry. Why are you tryin' to deny me food? Let's agree to disagree and talk later, if we have a later, and eat more of that crooked, ugly-ass food now. That bite tasted good. Can I have some more coffee too?"

Increasing the oil on the now fully hot, aged waffle iron, Zoe adds more batter. She pours two coffees, pausing to watch the oily swirl on top of the hot brew, and thinking about the two kinds of oil.

> *Maybe I need to order better filters. Is oil added to coffee beans? Is my water hot enough, or pure enough, or contaminated in some way? Fred and I would have talked about this; the ordinary things of life. I sure miss him.*

As they settle down to eat, Celtic music is playing this time, with Zoe imagining people walking on misty moors. "Danny Boy," a haunting song. Pipes calling Danny. Loss. Fred's death comes roiling in, another wave of memories and she thinks,

> *Seems there is so much silence around death and so much mind paid to birth. Two ends of the arc.*

Ruby Blue, picking up on Zoe's mood, offers, "Thank you for my special waffles. Guess we are both learning to be more open to hearing about each other's experiences."

> *Man, White people. She wasn't even listenin' to what I was sayin' or even took time to understand where I was comin' from. Seems like Black people always gotta follow the White rules without hesitation. You even gotta make sure they feel comfortable but then they actin' like we offend them with the truth of our experiences or ability to seek more answers. Devilish if you ask me, but I am feeling safe and fed right now, so I'm willin' to bite my tongue. But, if I do, am I giving up the real me? If so, it is for me and the baby.*

"Uh, you got a stamp I could have?"

"Sure, Ruby."

"And paper? And a envelope?"

"Sure."

"And could you put my letter in the mailbox, please?"

"Yes, Ruby."

With a smile, "It's for Marcus. And, to answer your question, nah, I would never call no police for help. Uniforms make me uneasy. Black men too often end up wearin' one. Prison. Fast Food. Military. They can take my freedom away. You know, truth is—if Black women were free, everyone would be free because our freedom would mean the systems of oppression had been destroyed."

Ruby Blue pauses, considering whether to continue with her comments, then decides to let it go. "Night, Zoe."

MARCUS

MARCUS

'm Marcus, named after Marcus Garvey. Check 'em out. His idea of separate but equal for the races makes sense to me. But I ain't moving to Liberia or some shit like that. Nah, not happenin'.

When I was a shorty, I was pretty much caught up in myself. I worked low-pay jobs to make money for tats and dying my hair, well, and art supplies. I told Ma I was independent in all ways, except financial. Before death caught up with her, she was proud of how handsome I am. And I know I'm sexy too. I wasn't focused on the future. But then I met my Ruby Blue and I fell in love with her. Man, I love her to death. And we got a baby on the way. Wanna know more? You gotta keep readin'. Later. Peace.

TEMPORARY FOSTER MOM?

Loud knocking on the bedroom door, "Ruby, Ruby, wake up. Eleanor called from the agency."

"I'm up, I'm up. I'll start packin'."

Don't no one care nothin' about me; all they want is my...

"Ruby, listen to me. First, she said your Covid test came back negative. We can ease up on the social distancing. And second, she said the shelters and social services are desperate to place young people like you. She asked if I would become your temporary foster mom for now; we can skip some of the usual qualifying procedures. What do you think?"

What am I saying? I don't really know much about this young woman, this serious, astute teenager, in trouble. She seems to be thoughtful and smart, but afraid. Well, I'm afraid too. This is a big commitment. What am I doing? This could be good; better than getting a cat. Well, and both things can happen. A family? Am I creating a temporary surrogate family? So fast? Fred would approve. Thanks, Fred. I'll go for it.

"Stop playin' with me, Zoe."

Wait. Wait. Listen, baby girl, we gotta catch our breath. What I gotta do? I gotta say okay to this. No other options.

"No, seriously, Ruby. I must go through a two-day Zoom training on the computer; nothing is face-to-face anymore with Covid. And then, even better, they will pay us to have you here, eating my crooked food."

"What I gotta do?"

"Just be here."

"Until the baby comes? What about Marcus?"

"We will see what happens with the father of your baby."

"Yeah."

"After his hearing, we will find out what his sentence is and then go from there. What do you think?"

"I hear you. Does this mean we can eat together at the kitchen table now?"

"Yes."

"I'm hungry…got anything for me to munch on or am I going to die of famine?"

"Well, come help me fix breakfast. You can wash the spinach for our omelets."

As Ruby Blue wraps the blue blanket around her shoulders, the women walk together down the short hallway to the kitchen, both thinking about what they are agreeing to. It is their first time being physically close.

Ruby Blue's eyes focus on the dull brown and yellow kitchen wallpaper, faded from many washings and lackluster from years of sunshine sneaking in the north-facing window, where an African violet, blooming deep purple, proudly rests with no water spots on its expansive leaves and Ruby Blue distractedly considers how healthy the plant looks. Thriving. While she reflects,

What do I want to do? What do I want to do? I need to think about my baby. I got to think about our safe space. It could be here.

Ruby Blue offers Zoe a long, slow, blinkless look, then reaches toward the bag of spinach.

Only for the baby. After she is born, I'm outta here. I'll figure out a way to get some bread. This foster cash could be good for me and Marcus and our little girl.

"Can we put some money on Marcus' books so he can call me?"

"Do you know how?" Zoe asks.

"Yeah, all but gettin' the money part."

"We will do that so you and Marcus can talk about your baby girl. And, we still think she is a girl?"

"Yeah, I know it in my heart. For sure."

"Maybe we should make a doctor's appointment for you now."

Ruby Blue pauses to consider going to see a doctor, remembering her great-auntie. A doctor did cure her decades-long foot pain. He found a tack completely buried in her heel. Then, "I probably could see a doctor. But that's nasty." A deep breath before Ruby Blue asks, "Eleanor pays, right?"

"We will make that work."

"Uh, do you have a safety pin I can use to hold my bra? My tits real big right now and aching."

"Yes, hon."

* * *

The women sit together at the round, oak kitchen table for the first time. The clock in the living room cuckoos slowly, resolutely. Nine. The chairs have matching brown cushions attached with corresponding laces. Ruby Blue notices the kitchen is warmer than the living room. The painted part of the walls is yellowish with that 1980s cutting-edge "Cuppa Joe" wallpaper border at the ceiling level and down the wall where there is no countertop. There are two matching nubby brown placemats, one for Zoe and one for Fred, Ruby Blue figures, but now Fred's is for her.

"Ruby …"

"Since I'm stayin, you should know I prefer to go by Ruby Blue."

"What?"

"If you don't want to add the Blue, then just call me Ms. Smith. You're a Smith too. Maybe my people were chattel for your people. To me, Smith is common, like Williams or Johnson or Jones or Brown or Jackson. But it's mine so I keep it."

"Smyth. I am Smyth, with a Y—the British spelling. I kept my maiden name when I married Fred," Zoe corrects.

"Yeah, okay," Ruby Blue explains. "Post slavery, some people renamed themselves, but the story is my family kept the White peoples' name, a so-called good Christian name. Ruby is a gem. Early, they treasured me for my baby beauty. I was told that many families changed their names to Freeman or Freedman and the like. But others kept the plantation name in hopes of being able to reunite with family that was sold or separated by slavery. An odd kind of leash (or whip) that connects families.

Stopping to take a drink of coffee, Ruby Blue then continues. "You ever notice that African Americans don't ask each other's names as much as they ask about who their kin are? Because our families were so divided and disconnected and sold willy-nilly, and our women legally raped by White men, we call each other bro(ther) or sis or cuz or uncle or auntie even when we don't know if we are blood-related. We're still family. So, Ruby Smith. And my man added in the Blue, so Ruby Blue Smith. That is my name."

"Thanks for all this explanation, Ruby Blue. I will remember. You are a good teacher."

"Guess this coffee cup wallpaper is what makes me want coffee all the time. Aretha! Thanks for playing her. *She say a little prayer...*"

"YouTube is magic."

"Oh, how I love him. No one but him. I believe." Ruby Blue sways with the music.

"Tell me about your man, about Marcus."

Sensing the opportunity for a deeper conversation, both women relax into the moment, "I will if you will tell me about your baby's daddy. I assume it wasn't Fred, right?"

A CALL AT NO COST TO YOU

THIS IS A CALL AT NO COST TO YOU FROM THE COUNTY JAIL. WILL YOU ACCEPT IT? SAY YES OR PRESS 5.

"Yes."

ALL CALLS, OTHER THAN PROPERLY PLACED ATTORNEY CALLS, MAY BE MONITORED AND RECORDED.

Zoe quickly hands the phone to Ruby Blue.

"Hey, baby!" she whispers.

"Hey, you, my Ruby Blue. We a mess and I know you makin' that troubled, terrible face right now. There's so much going on the backside, but on the front, we just keep puttin' one foot in front of the other. Are you stayin' safe?"

"Yeah, I'm keepin' me and our baby safe. Those people left me high and dry. Stole the stimulus debit cards and never looked back. Hell. They just split. They goddam sho ain't no kin of mine. They didn't have to do me dirty like that. If you were here, I know we would be good." Ruby Blue's voice cracks as she tears up.

Marcus, sensing the tears, soothes her, "It's okay to cry. You have to cry or you can't get over it, you just get through it, Baby. You ain't used to be this angry. We are family and if I messed up, I messed you up too. Don't be scared; it'll work out. I'll make good this time."

Lowering her voice, "Baby, I got no one but this old woman. I can't believe I slept on their dirty couch for three nights before I got here, if you call that sleep. I didn't want to be trouble to anyone but everybody has to be trouble to somebody, right. I got to think about the baby."

"Good you called 2-1-1. People at the agency must be in your corner. Our corner. They got you to the old woman, right?"

ALL CALLS, OTHER THAN PROPERLY PLACED ATTORNEY CALLS, MAY BE MONITORED AND RECORDED.

"Damn I hate them listenin'. Will there ever be a time when we can be alone with no White people near? I have made up my mind to live all I can while I can; I'm a grown woman and soon to be a mother. I want to make something for our daughter..."

YOU HAVE ONE MINUTE REMAINING.

"Hell yes, but for now, we will make this work, Baby. Don't be afraid."

"Ouch. When I have a stomach ache, drinkin' a little soda helps it go away. I need some soda right now. But this lady won't let me have none."

Ruby Blue turns around and smirks at Zoe, who smiles back, holding up a tea bag.

"You on the streets is a no-go, Baby. You gotta stay with the old woman."

"Ok, that'll work, but I'm not to be played with. But, I'm good. You good, Baby? Love..."

DIAL TONE

MY BLACK KING

Ruby Blue stands and gently places the phone back on the wall receiver and silently looks out at the sunrise coming through the east living room window, thinking about the overly brief phone call and how she is missing her Black King, Marcus.

> *So often, my man, I wish I could send you images from my brain, my Black King. If I could, I'd send a picture of the tangerine morning sun rising. Such beauty. I notice the beauty in the world more fully, more completely, knowing I need to hold that in my heart for the artist in you, my Marcus.*

Picking up a piece of now-cold toast, Zoe changes the subject, again. "Right. But let's start with your love, Marcus, before we talk about my baby's father. Is his name special too?"

"Might be."

"And?"

"Love is a close readin'. Yeah. My man is the color of coffee diluted with cream. Lighter than me." Ruby Blue pauses, suddenly wondering.

> *Is that just another -ism: nationalism, shadism, racism, agism,?*

"Well, even though it's wrong, the hierarchy based on skin tone is real. Our baby will be too. Light. Her beauty won't be trampled by having a blue-black dad who is defined by what he is not, lighter skinned. My Granny was always yelling at me to wear a hat when I was a girl. She believed that things like drinkin' coffee and eatin' chocolate while carrying a baby would turn the child dark. I hope that ain't true, 'cause I do love me some coffee. I remember seein' a homely baby and someone sayin', 'Oh, bless her little heart; she'll grow into her looks." Ruby Blue pauses again, reflecting.

Do I need to apologize for these feelings? Allow our daughter to be unapologetically Black? I just want her to be safe. It's dangerous for us in this jungle.

"Our baby will have Marcus' big smiling disk eyes, filled with lights. His eyes and his smile give 'way his emotions, like lovin' me. She'll have a wide African nose like he and I both have."

Smiling shyly, Ruby Blue continues, "He has a tall, strong, beautiful body with lots of crimson and blue tats."

Ooohh, I love his tats. And I love his brown skin.

"He has hieroglyphic shapes on his right arm and clouds on his left, all the way to his elbows. We have matchin' ankh symbols, half on my right hand and half on his left. Together they represent us, one life we have created together. Sometimes I would trace them with my fingers when we made love. I miss that."

I miss him.

"He has a star on his left breast—maybe it is meant to resemble his heart. There are lines and patterns around the star from his chest up to his shoulders. Earrings, both ears, that match my nose ring. We got 'em together. And his hair? Natural but dyed blond and maybe eight inches long although

I wonder what it looks like now that he's in jail. When he is free, he moves like a cat, real swift, always on the balls of his feet. You'd never be able to catch him lackin'."

"You have given him a close read," Zoe encourages.

"Yeah, we real in-tune. Marcus is different than my daddy was before he left. Daddy was not a settlin' man, as they say, the victim of a carefree life and those policies that keep Black men out of the home. After prison, he couldn't live with my mom and me in the public housing. Prohibited. I loved my dad and he loved him(self) too, so we loved the same person. I think his key to stayin' lost was never to really love anyone, other than himself. His mom did her best to raise him, but you know how shorties wanna test the hood, as Common says. He was street; loved to bang. His penis was his best friend, his brain. I think Daddy mostly woke up in some stranger's bed. Might as well call him a rollin' stone.

"Not Marcus.

"Marcus is a big, strong guy. A target. You cannot be a big Black man with a solid build and not get pulled over by the police regularly. And he wears bright colors all the time, specifically different shades of pink, which makes him even more of a target. I love him even more for it; he doesn't allow others to dictate his decisions. I read a sentence from Nina Simone that fit for him (and me) and it stuck; defined my fear. She said somethin' like, *The fear that comes with realizing one's humanity is criminalized, threatening, and expendable often drives many Black people into a subdued existence.*

"Too many see him as dangerous, which is part of why I'd never go to a cop for help. War on Drugs added to that fear on both sides. But they don't know him like I do with my close readin'. He hides his emotions with people, other than me. He gives others a bland face, 'bout as emotional as algebra. He is constantly wearing a mask. Who can blame him, livin' in a world that doesn't respect him as a man. That sees him as *expendable*. What a word."

Zoe refills the coffee cups. "Go on, Ruby Blue, I'm listening."

"In bed, we like prisoners in solitary, downin' our rations of bread and water. We couldn't get enough. The first one to light my fuse. My one and only." Ruby Blue smiles slowly, remembering.

> *I love how my cheeks still hurt so good when I'm*
> *thinking about you, my man.*

"I was around twelve when I started gettin' tits and bleeding. Suddenly, I felt like a body surrounded by my pussy. At least that is how men looked at me, like they hadn't been neutered. They wanted me to be a lady in the streets and a freak in the sheets. They had to wear their desire so openly, it was embarrassing, humiliatin' that they were not able to hide what they wanted.

"That wasn't for me. I was shy. Marcus liked that; no, he loved that. He knew I was his, and he was mine. I was hooked into him like a tick; swollen with love for him. I could taste the sugar and salt from his lips. I could smell that faint, intimate odor of his body that lingered on mine after we were together. I can smell it now on his hoodie. That is the last thing I have of his."

Ruby Blue runs her hand, caressingly, up and down her arm, along the sleeve of the hoodie she now wears most of the time. "I remember touching the rise of his chest and arms. He played me, but not in a *played me* way. I mean he knew how to play my body like a violin until I'd melt, moving, trembling into him. Locked into him. My heart decided to love him first, then my brain. Who tells Black men they are loved? Not society. Not the media. The only people who truly know how to love Black men are Black women. Shared journey. This baby will be the lovin' proof of our intimacy. I know we are young, but this love we share is old."

Turning and changing her wistful gaze from the beauty outside the window, Zoe pauses, then says, "That is a poem, Ruby Blue. A ballad. I used to teach English and you are a poet. I envy the love you two have. And your baby girl is going to be so lucky to have you both."

"Thanks, Zoe. And now I'll take a nap and maybe write my man."

3AM

There is a rapid, frightened knocking on her bedroom door. Ruby Blue bursts into the dark room and grabs Zoe's hand.

Is that you, Fred? Wait, you're dead. Why is it always 3am when things go wrong?

"What, Ruby Blue?"

"I don't feel right. Somethin's wrong. I'm so scared."

Sitting up and consciously pulling her pajama top together covering her sagging breasts, Zoe invites, "Come and sit on the bed. Tell me what you are feeling."

"My heart's beating fast. Real fast. Too fast! My head hurts. And, my stomach hurts; like a sharp pain, almost as if I'm being stabbed."

Reaching out, Zoe touches Ruby Blue's arm with concern, laced with care. And gentleness.

Same situation with Fred. 3am. A touch. And then he died. That isn't going to happen this time.

Softly, "Take a deep breath and sit up real straight, hon. See if that helps."

"Zoe, I don't do hospitals and I damn sho don't do no doctors if I can help it."

I'm real afraid. We need help. But I know Zoe will help us. I am sure of it. She knows what to do.

"Okay, get a coat from my closet and we will go to the emergency room. Just when we were going to make a doctor's appointment, you take the fast track!"

"No teasing right now, Zoe. I need you to be serious."

"You are right, Ruby Blue. Out to the car."

Damn, I hope this car starts. It hasn't been run in weeks because there is literally nowhere to go. Geeze, they even gave us an auto insurance rebate because we collectively weren't driving much during this pandemic.

As Ruby Blue pulls the seatbelt around her, shivering, Zoe reassures her. "It will take us about ten minutes to get to the hospital. They won't let me come in with you, I don't think. But we will try. If I can't come in, know that I will wait in the parking lot for you for however long it takes. I'll write my phone number down."

"I know your phone number 'cause I gave it to Marcus. I gave him your address so he can write me. I hope that's okay."

"It's okay, Ruby Blue."

What! She sent my address into the jail without asking me! Later, we will talk about that.

"Let's fix this fast heart first. One thing at a time. Keep taking deep breaths, blow the air out slowly through your mouth, and all the way to the end. Try to relax."

Zoe slows her breathing as she tries to demonstrate the technique and consciously calm herself at the same time, while pushing the start button on the car and gratefully hearing the engine beep—the hybrid starter sound. Mechanically, she backs out of her one-car garage and down the short driveway, as she has done for decades.

She glances at Ruby Blue, whose fear is visceral—gut level—as she sits with her hands caressing the bulge of her stomach, yet quivering with dread. It is too early in the pregnancy for any sort of complication. And the women silently share the fear of going to the hospital where so many people have gone these days and never left. Alive, that is. Like Fred. Zoe thinks,

Don't lose this baby. Don't miscarry. Don't.

Glancing over at Ruby Blue as a corner streetlight brightens the car, "Yes, breathe deeply, in through your nose, then blow the breath all the way out through your mouth. Good. Good. Slow. This is Qigong, you know. You are doing it. I'll teach you more Qigong when we get back home that will help when your baby is being born. Qigong is similar to yoga, but gentler. I know you want to know all of this right now. Just teasing." Zoe places a comforting hand on the anxious teen's shoulder and feels the tight muscles soften a bit.

"For now, just concentrate on you. I'll chat on; you think about slow breathing. You are going..."

Rattled, Ruby Blue blurts out, "How do I pay for this? I don't have any money. You won't leave me, right? You betta not leave me. You betta not leave us!"

"I won't leave you, Ruby Blue, and we will work on medical payment later. First, we need to get you well."

They pull up to the emergency entrance, seeing the line of refrigerator trucks parked to the side, and call the number written large on the door. The questions come, "Are you experiencing shortness of breath..."

Come on. Come on. Fred was in this same hospital. So many Covid patients. So many hospitals have these trailers parked outside to stack all the dead bodies. I see the pictures on TV. This is terrifying. I can't let Ruby Blue see how scared I am; I just lost the only other person in my life. Hum, I hadn't thought about Ruby Blue in this way before, as a significant person in my life already in only a few days. I have done some reading on the very high rates of troubled pregnancies among Black girls and women. I need to learn more. She will be okay. She will be fine. She won't need a respirator. She is resilient.

Responding to the disconnected, tinny voice, "No. No Covid symptoms."

The voice instructs, "Stay in your car and we will come to you." It is like a disembodied voice from God. Maybe s/he does reside in the hospital emergency entrances these days.

A person, standing at the car window and dressed in full protective gear asks again, "Is she having symptoms of shortness of breath, high fever, a cough, headache?"

Impatiently, Zoe snaps, "You just asked us that."

I should respectfully be letting Ruby Blue speak for herself. Next time.

"No. She is six or seven months pregnant, and her heart is racing. I will wait for her in the car because I know I can't come in, right?"

"Correct."

"What's your name, young lady?" the person asks.

"Ruby. Ruby Blue."

* * *

The minutes pass and, after sitting in her car for nearly an hour with the engine running to provide some heat, Zoe's phone rings. The sound is startling even though it is what she has been waiting for.

"ZOE, ZOE, THEY SAY THEY KEEPIN' ME IN THE HOSPITAL ALL DAY. I AIN'T GOIN' FOR IT!"

"Breathe, Ruby Blue. Is your doctor there right now? May I talk with her or him?"

"She's gone. She says preeclampsia. That's what my momma had. Dead. Death can make you wish you'd never been born."

"You're sweet, Ruby Blue. Poetic, as I said, but you are in good medical hands now and you are not going to die. What is your doctor's name? I'll call her and see what we need to do. Ruby Blue, I won't leave you. I'll do that virtual training now and then we are going to be together officially. Temporary fostering. Although I sometimes think it is you who is fostering me. Try not to worry. I am afraid all your worry and stress are factors in this, so we are going to work on taking care of that too. Okay?"

"Okay. Okay. Her name is Dr. Foster. Funny. You fosterin' me and she is fosterin' me."

* * *

That afternoon, Zoe again sits in her car in the hospital parking lot, staring at the hygienic sign, "Call 800 222 6000 for instructions. Stay in your car. Masking is required at all times."

Soon she will be called to drive to the front of the hospital to pick up Ruby Blue.

What have I gotten myself into? Do I want to commit to this young woman and all her problems? Have I already committed with the fostering, which will include the birth of her baby. Am I afraid for her?

I am no longer afraid OF her.

Does she have any idea what she is facing with childbirth? Women do protect each other from the throes of that experience. She is young, like I was. Childbirth was a turning point in my life. I became a woman; never naïve again. Full grown. Different than my peers forevermore. What will Ruby Blue face? Am I able to help or guide, or even listen, to her? How? Which of us is more frightened? I wonder…and then a baby. A baby she will be able to keep, and love.

Zoe watches the wheelchair come through the hospital side-door exit. A nurse clumsily helps Ruby Blue into the car, seemingly afraid to touch her. Zoe wonders,

Covid? Race? Or both?

Reaching back to pull, then fasten, her seat belt, Ruby Blue sighed, "Zoe, you came back."

Relieved, Zoe smiles and nods. "Yes, I'm here. Dr. Foster told me you have what is called mild preeclampsia. Your blood pressure is 140/90, which is high, but not through the roof. I told Dr. Foster I am your foster parent, so she is letting you come home with me. No hospital stay. We are going to do lots of research on this and then regular medical visits. We are going to cut out salt and add eight glasses of water daily. We are going to get more of that chicken into you. You liked that chicken dish I made, right? And guess what? You are going to be lying on your left side, mostly in bed, from now on."

"I can't do that, catch y'all's breath. Why?" Ruby Blue takes a long breath, "Can I do that? I guess if I got to. You gonna feed me? I know what you bought to feed me. That raw spinach!"

"You can do this. WE are going to do this."

> *Thank you, Covid. In a strange way, with Fred gone and no more teaching, it seems I am in just the right place to take care of this child 24/7. And I am realizing I want to. Where did that come from?*

Quizzically, Ruby Blue asks, "Why lie on my left side? That some kind of voodoo?"

"This is true in yoga too. We rest on our left sides to take pressure off major blood vessels, Dr. Foster told me. I do it because I'm old. You will be doing it to keep your baby's weight from pressing on those vessels. Did you find out your baby's gender?"

Wrinkling up her nose, "You don't know what that Dr. Foster did to me. All nasty and embarrassing. Cold and invasive, but she tried to be gentle. And, yes, my baby is a girl. I already told you I knew that."

> *Actually, I do know what Dr. Foster did, but how do I tell Ruby Blue? I'm glad it was done kindly. That wasn't my experience.*

"Yes, you did know she was going to be a girl. One of these days, we will talk about what you and Marcus are going to name her."

Twisting in the car seat and reaching out, slowly, taking Zoe's hand in both of hers, "How about Zoe? How about if I call my baby girl Zoe?"

"Oh, Ruby Blue. That's very flattering of you to consider. But, let's see what Marcus wants to do; he is in on this too."

Literally.

"This is just wrong. I do all the work and he gets to lie around in a warm, comfy bed with people feeding him."

"Hum, I doubt his bed is comfy, but the rest sounds kind of like what you are going to be doing for the next couple of months!"

"You evil ol' woman." Her half-smile and shoulder shrug kid Zoe.

Zoe chuckles, starts the car, and puts her fingers up to her head to resemble horns.

BED REST

It is a cool spring morning. Flecks of snow mingle with rain. The grass in my yard is alive and smiling. Greening. It knows nothing of a pandemic.

So much has changed in our collective human lives with this Covid. I miss the simple things—things that were unproblematic for me—like a walk to the bakery on a sunny spring morning. Exercise and an extra fine, still warm, donut.

I sit, looking out the bedroom window while putting on my Van Gogh socks, the ones I gave my sister because she loved Starry Night, but then took back after she died, when I was helping clean out her house. The socks are warm for this cool morning. Swirls of yellow and orange.

As I put them on, I realize Ruby Blue knows nothing of the patchwork history that fills my life spaces. Parents gone. Sister gone. Brother-in-law gone. Fred gone. So many people gone and yet their memories and links fill my life still. We are collections of our lived experiences that shape how we interact with the world and, I guess, what we see when we view it. This is true for Ruby Blue too.

Well, just put the Van Gogh socks on and move forward.

The spare bedroom, where Ruby Blue is staying, doubled as an office. Journals from past adventures Zoe had taken and books of various sizes and colors and widths fill two matching bookcases. Neatly. The books are arranged by subject rather than by color, which is something Zoe has been seeing, with amusement, as backdrops behind some TV pundits who speak with authority about the pandemic and the protests, both of which are filling the newscasts. Ruby Blue has unceremoniously pushed two decorative bed pillows on the floor.

Zoe remembers the triangular reading pillow in the basement. She used it over the years for propping herself up all cozy in bed to read student papers and prepare lectures. What is going to be needed for Ruby Blue's bed rest and is it okay to bring that pillow up from Fred's bed? It has been weeks since he died but did that Covid virus linger longer on fabric? She'd check this out. She had barely ventured into the basement since Fred's death.

Dr. Foster suggested a pregnancy pillow, which turned out to be a soft, C-shaped whole-body cushion that Zoe ordered online.

The one thing that works extraordinarily well during these Covid times is home delivery.

Zoe always leaves a tip for the regular local essential worker who has been enacting his Willie Nelson façade with beard, braids, and red bandana carefully folded to show the word, *Crazy*. Plus, a mask, of course. What is going to happen when people's pent-up demand—hobby, actually—for in-person shopping is rekindled when this pandemic fades, she wonders.

Two Covid vaccines are in the process of being approved for emergency use. Too late for Fred, but Zoe knows she will get vaccinated in the early wave, being a strong believer in preventive healthcare, and knowing there are some benefits to being old. No information is available yet on possible dangers for vaccinating pregnant women. Researchers just don't know.

The hospital stay and prenatal explorations have sobered Ruby Blue. She is still resisting the situation, but is now more resigned, although still tentative about the restraints put on her, and being in this stranger's home. Is she truly safe? Is the offered support real? It seems to be, on the surface. But what does Zoe get out of helping her? A mystery. Where else could she go, and now with this preeclampsia diagnosis. Out of choices. Stay steady; just follow the path. No way to deal with all the issues she and Marcus face; just deal with the immediate difficulties. Yep, there is more to life than just having a good time all the damn time.

"I got your room set up for this bed rest, Ruby Blue. I've ordered a pregnancy pillow and this reading pillow will prop you up for now."

"What am I supposed to do all day and all night? There isn't even a TV in this room and barely one in the living room. I have to squint my eyes just to see it. You read too many damn books. Is that what I am to be stuck doing? Sleepin'. Eatin'. Readin'. And that's all!"

"Some would die for this opportunity, Ruby Blue."

Ruby Blue thinks, *And I ain't gonna be one of them.*

Zoe thinks, *Hum, a phrase I shouldn't be using any more: To die for an opportunity.*

"Two or three months of being catered to and having time to read and be. It is an introvert's dream."

"Not me. I ain't no introvert. There's good and this ain't it. And I ain't dyin'."

"Well, you don't have any choice, about the bed rest, I mean. It's either stay here with me and follow Dr. Foster's rules or go to the hospital for the rest of your pregnancy. I guess you decide. Homeless on the street is not a good choice for you and your baby girl."

Ruby Blue sits down on the bed laboriously, brow furrowed, and puts her hands on both sides of her face, then slides them down in what could be a prayer position covering her mouth. "I know. I get it. I ain't stupid. Damn. I wish Marcus could call. I wanna sleep now. Leave me alone."

Yes, damn it. Why am I trying here? Sometimes I get angry with this petulant child. She lashes out at me like her (many) issues are my problem, my fault. I am trying. I am trying from my heart. I know I'm making mistakes in understanding. I know it isn't Ruby Blue's job to teach me. Maybe I should just stop caring at all, except I am a grown and compassionate woman and know enough not to give up based on one incident, one event.

She really has no idea what she is facing, from the pregnancy, the jailed boyfriend, their lack of formal education, and job history—what IS their formal education and work history—to the hospital bills, to the statistical very real danger of death for her or her baby.

And what will happen after this baby is born? She doesn't know and I will protect her from thinking about these things right now because that is what grown-ups do. Still, these arrows of hers hurt and I truly don't think I deserve them. Well, we will just have a little distance and then come back at this situation from a new angle. I need to be the adult. But, damn, she does piss me off. Geeze, I'm speaking like her now.

* * *

"Ruby Blue, dinner's ready."

"You mean I get to walk all the way into the kitchen? You gonna Granny-troll me now?"

Turning quickly, brow furrowed, "Ruby Blue. That is enough. You do not get to talk to me this way. It is not my fault that you—and I—need to have you stay very still for two or so months. It just is. I know you are frustrated. I get it."

Long pause as Ruby Blue looks at the chicken casserole and spinach on the table and wrinkles her nose.

Eww, what the hell is this?

Dispirited, "You right. My Granny, wit' her head tied up in a scarf, would have said, 'I'll slap the black off you.' I'm sorry."

"This is hard for both of us, and harder for you. A bad patch, for sure. I understand why you want to talk with Marcus and maybe he will call tonight. As we know, he doesn't have control over what he can do in the jail. So, anyway, here is a chicken casserole with spinach, lime, and cilantro for taste. We are not doing salt anymore; we will have to change our taste buds. We will do this together. No complaining! I ordered some salmon for delivery tomorrow and I'll make a zucchini bread. There is a whole preeclampsia diet that Dr. Foster told me about, for us. So, you eat and drink that water. No complaining from here on out, unless you really need to!"

Silence echoes in the kitchen. Zoe fills the space, "Books. Yes, I have many books and I love books. They feel and smell good. My mother used to take me to the local library. She did not like the fact that books had to be returned in two weeks, so she made me take them out the back door for her. Steal them. We always returned them, which was almost as challenging as sneaking them out, but it might have been a month or even longer. She tried to start me on a criminal career."

Sullenly. "Folks be like that," Ruby Blue mutters.

"Hum, I guess that isn't very funny given that Marcus is in jail for theft. You see how insensitive I can be. I forget stuff. Sorry."

Ruby Blue nodding, "That's okay. Chicken's good."

Working to fill the silence and wondering why she didn't play some music, Zoe asks, "Do you like to read?"

"Yes, I do. Did. I haven't had time for that in quite a while. Maybe now. Speaking of books, can we put some more money on Marcus' books at the jail so he can call me? It doesn't seem to be workin'."

"Sure. We will figure that out in the morning. Sleep well."

Ruby Blue heads down the hall while Zoe stacks the dinner dishes, thinking back to her mother's admonitions never to stack dirty dishes, getting both the top and bottom soiled and making more work for the dishwasher—person or machine. Then she consciously stacks the dessert dishes. When all are placed in the dishwasher, Zoe moves to her favorite chair with the good reading light. Sitting. What a day! Yes, a wearying day. It would have been the perfect time to have a lazy cat for company and spend this early spring day watching the daylight hours extend, and simply retreating into a book. Cozy. Sleepy.

* * *

"Good morning, Ms. Smith! A fine day it is for morning people. And here is the first of your eight glasses of water for the day. Time to get up."

"Look, I'm a fragile and fallen human being. Don't force your morning sunshine on me."

Zoe responds to Ruby Blue's comment. "Not accepting delivery—ha ha, that's a little pregnancy joke. We will be awake and chipper and have water, oatmeal, and blueberries for breakfast. Yes, and coffee!"

"Oh, you so woke." Seeing the sun, Ruby Blue narrows her eyes and grimaces.

"Sleep. Eat. Sleep. Eat. Drink water. Eat. And it has only been a few days!"

Cheerily nodding toward a white board Zoe had used in her teaching, she says, "I found this great idea on the Internet for things to do during bedrest. A vision board! Are you artistic? We could make a board that lets you imagine your, and Marcus, and the baby's futures.

"What kind of job or careers do you want? What kind of cars do you want to drive? A house? An apartment? Schooling? Travel? What do you imagine for your baby? The article said to look at the board daily and add to or delete from it. Stay positive. Stay focused. You can make your dreams come true! What do you think?"

Leaning heavily on her left side against the triangular pillow, Ruby Blue mutters, "Let's just pull out my fingernails instead. This pandemic is supposed to be the great equalizer, right? Everyone affected the same. Well, not. That is why those people I was livin' with left. Minimum wage, even with three of them essential workers—like lots of Black and Brown people. Informal jobs, like under-the-counter cash. They hustle and still don't make it. Their jobs overlapped so someone was always stayin' with the kids, but Internet access was unreliable so the kids couldn't do their schoolwork and did not get free lunches any more. They were bored. The parents weren't eatin' sometimes and givin' the food to the kids. They were hopin' for $600 relief money for each of them and then they don't need to work at all, especially those who had felonies on their records and had trouble getting any legit work. Dreams for the future?

"The school gave the kids a laptop, which was good, but they couldn't complain about the bad WiFi because they were all violatin' apartment rules. That one chick did have a felony record. And then the dude rear-ended the car and just ran away. He left his unlicensed car right there in the street. But even if they found him, he probably got warrants and no money, so wouldn't have paid the damage anyway. Collectively, we did not have an extra $500 for even minimal repairs to get the thing runnin' again."

"That's why they left you?" Zoe questions.

"Yeah, and did not pay the rent so I had to run too. I read that Black women make about half as much as White men, for the same kinds of jobs. That's messed up."

"Sixty-three cents on a dollar—that was on the news last night," Zoe recalls.

"You could see that on your tiny-ass TV screen?" Ruby Blue glances at Zoe, then quickly adds, "Teasing you. Don't get that look on your face. we just havin' fun. Don't you think that everyone should get respect for the hard work they do?

I'm a right good worker when I got a mind. I do my best, I really do."

Ruby Blue adjusts the triangular pillow, creating a circular cocoon between it and the pregnancy pillow, but not getting out of bed, yet.

"What am I about to put on that vision board? Dodge those who have power over our possibilities? Married to Marcus and he got a good job? Me in college. Three beautiful Black daughters all doin' well in school and not growin' up in the streets with too much crime? Kids not bein' shot by the cops? Marcus not bein' shot by the cops? Inheritin' tokens from Grandma like yo velvet striped chair and yo rosy sugar bowl? If you ain't got boots, it's hard to pull yourself up by your bootstraps. I read that somewhere, but it's true. One key to success is having parents and grandparents who succeeded. You know, Black Americans played a major role in building this country, but now don't have access to much of that wealth and resources."

Zoe adds, "Same news story on my tiny-ass TV last night said that for every $100 of wealth for White families in the U.S., Black families have the equivalent of about $5. Some-time, let's talk more about why that is."

Turning toward the white board, Ruby Blue replies, "I can tell you one thing that's gonna go on that vision board of mine. If my dreams come true, I won't be one who forgets. I won't be one who finds a place for themselves and forgets the ones on the bottom."

"For sure. And I'll leave you this pitcher of water to finish off today. Right! Breakfast in fifteen minutes."

"Yeah, yeah, yeah. I hear you." Zoe watches as Ruby Blue leans back onto the triangular pillow trying to get comfortable, her elbows on her raised knees in a position that allows her stomach to rest between her legs. Pensive. As she leaves the bedroom, Zoe wonders what Ruby Blue is feeling. Frustrated? Lethargic? Angry? Ensnared? She isn't quite sure but maybe some combination of all of these. Tired. That is for sure. Tired of all of this, and it is just starting.

ZOE FLASHBACK

Seeing Ruby Blue on that triangular pillow, I remember my mother as she tried to hide the shame of my teenage pregnancy, keeping me in my bedroom for two months. I wasn't allowed to go downstairs or even walk around where neighbors might see me through windows, all obviously and shamefully pregnant.

At one point, she wanted one of my boyfriends, not the baby's father, to see me and report back to others that, yes, in fact, I had mono, as the school officials had been told. The kissing disease. Infectious mononucleosis. A virus.

She propped me up in bed, leaning back on a triangular pillow. She positioned my knees to cover up my stomach, then concealed even that with blankets. Careful orchestration. The boy was allowed, very briefly, to visit me but not get too close. And so, the deception was spread by the teenage grapevine.

And then I was sent away to The Home.

PREECLAMPSIA

Later, after breakfast, Zoe returns to the bedroom to refresh the water.

Ruby Blue has clearly been pondering between naps. "Zoe, what does preeclampsia mean? What did I do to make this happen? Anything? The devil was always busy in my family. Was it because we lived in that dirty place with them others smoking and all?"

Zoe interrupts, "I'm not sure, Ruby Blue, but I did read more about it. First, you did not cause it, although your stress these past weeks may have added to the threat. But mostly it means you have high blood pressure—your blood is pulsing too strongly against your artery walls."

Extending her hand, Zoe says, "See the veins on the back of my hand? Yours don't show up the same way but imagine that there is too much pressure inside. Like a balloon blown too big. It is a complication from your pregnancy. The swelling in your ankles is a symptom. So is your fast heart rate. There is some danger to you and your baby, which is why this bed rest is so critical and is why we are going to the doctor every other week, with Zoom medical visits on other days, each week. It may be why you are so tired too. Your body is just asking you to take it easy. It is giving everything it can to your baby. We will monitor your blood pressure with the cuff Fred had."

Ruby Blue gives Zoe a worried look. Zoe responds, "It is okay for us to use it, even though he had Covid. The virus only lives a couple of days on fabric, versus a week or so on hard surfaces, they are saying now. So, we are good; Fred died a long time ago now and was in the hospital even before he died. But, back to your high blood pressure. It is very, very good we found out about this now. You were right to talk about your symptoms when you did. It is dangerous when not being treated." But we are handling it right and so very carefully. You and your baby are treasures to be held with care and love!"

"Aw, you ain't playin' with me, right."

"Nope," Zoe shakes her head and feels her hair shift in unusual ways.

I wish I could get a real haircut, at a beauty shop.

Repositioning to be able to breathe more easily around the baby pushing on her diaphragm, "So, tell me about your pregnancy."

"Ruby Blue!"

"No, for real. You promised you would if I told you about my love for Marcus."

Zoe looks down and away, pauses, takes a deep breath, then slowly replies, "Well, okay. My story was much like yours. I was 17 when I got pregnant. Unmarried, just like you. And I loved my guy. We dated off and on for two years, steadily when he wasn't cheating on me and seeing other girls. I should have dismissed him and gotten a good solid hobby. Horseback riding, which I loved, would have been respectable. Ironically, my mother said it was too sexual. I laugh at that now. There were no girl's athletics in the schools then, but if there had been, I'd have been fully involved in something, maybe baseball, maybe track. I was well coordinated and a lightning-fast runner."

Pausing and looking out the window while considering what to say next, Zoe gains courage from Ruby Blue's very open description of her relationship with Marcus.

"My guy and I kept flirting on the edge of actual full-bore intercourse, but stopping just in time. Exhausting! Then, one cloudy night, pretzeled in the back of his mother's beige Oldsmobile, with the windows steamed up, we just did not stop. Raw lust. Neither of us pulled back. No more his fault than mine. It was my first true, world-stopping, mind-blowing orgasm. I am certain our baby was conceived that night." Zoe slowly nods but doesn't make eye contact with Ruby Blue.

"There is a photo of me taken that summer. Sitting with my long hair tumbling around my shoulders, a jaunty scarf at my neckline. Suntanned and smiling. Mischievous. Looking at that photo, I see the last picture of me as a girl. I would never again be her. The harm had been done.

"A couple of months later, the knot in my gut felt like the omen of our social failure. When I told my guy I thought I might be pregnant, the words hung in the air like a heavy chain on my neck. He went far away to college and left me alone. I did not see him again for 25 years."

Deciding on the path to follow for her story, Zoe adds, "On a business trip, all those years later, I made my first journey ever to the town he lived in—where he had gone away to college. I looked him up in the phone book, which was the way things were done then. His name was there. I wrote down his number on hotel note paper and carried it around in my pocket for two days, deciding. Should I call? Ours had not been a casual fling. In spite of the drama, I believe it was the first real love for both of us.

Gesturing as if dialing an old-fashioned rotary phone, Zoe continues, "As I dialed his number, my hands shook so badly I had to stop, regroup, and then dial again.

"He answered the phone. I recognized his voice, and he, mine. Did he want to meet? Yes.

"He came to my hotel to pick me up and take me back to his home where his wife, ironically also named Zoe, was preparing dinner for us all. He called my room, and we met in the lobby. It was one of those large tubular hotels where the core is open 12 or 15 stories, with glass elevators, so we saw each other before talking. Sounds were echoey, hollow in that artificial setting."

"What do you say after such a long time? Shit, that's longer than I have been alive!" Ruby Blue blurts out. She was listening, imagining the scene.

"Exactly. What do you say to a long-ago lover after 25 years? A hello. An awkward, yet intimate, hug that felt surprisingly comforting and familiar. In spite of a vague sense of shame, I could feel a wash of that first attraction I had felt for him from day one. He was the new guy in my high school with his long wavey hair, leather boots, and Honda RC166 motorcycle, which turned out not to be his.

"Then his first question in the hotel lobby. Did I want to go back upstairs to my room with him? Although that was a flattering invitation, so quickly offered after so many years, I declined. We climbed into his rusted Volvo and drove toward his home among scrubby piñon trees. After the traffic thinned, his second question came. 'Were you pregnant?' The question was jolting. If he had truly suspected that, why hadn't he asked me 25 years before?

"I said yes and told him that I had given birth to our son, who had been adopted. He did not ask for more detail and offered no apology for having left me alone to deal with the upshot of our sex, which, I suppose, was biologically accurate. Perhaps just a semen volley to him. It seemed he thought of our baby in those terms, but was not at all curious about what the child, my parents, and I had gone through. He did offer that he and his Zoe had four children, and then hesitantly added, in his only response to my having been pregnant, 'I was terribly young.'

"I guess that answered the question of whether I should have tried to keep the baby and raise him. I'd have been alone." Zoe shakes her head. Thinking back.

"The pregnancy was a bad time for me and my parents, Ruby Blue. Mom and Dad were so disappointed with me. Anger would have been easier. In the 1960s, being pregnant without being married was considered a dreadful thing; a violation of social hopes and dreams when a two-parent, two-gender family with two to three children was the aim. I was sent away to that home for unwed mothers, as they were called then."

Seeing Ruby Blue's eyes half close, Zoe pauses, "How is that for a start to the story?"

"More to come? You promise?"

"Sure, but now you need to rest."

"Is it okay if I look at some of your books on the shelves over there?"

"Yes, just keep lying on your left side whenever you can and drinking that water."

"Right. I ain't playin' no mo'."

VIKISITA

After hearing Ruby Blue make another bathroom trip, Zoe walks into the bedroom and sits on the bedside. "I just read more about this and wrote it down because I couldn't figure out why lying on your left side was such a good thing, Ruby Blue. Here it is, 'Lying on your left side improves circulation, giving nutrient-packed blood an easier route from your heart to the placenta to nourish your baby.' If we can believe the Internet, and sometimes we can, I think, this is useful information. It is easier to follow-through with a plan when you know the *why*."

Gesturing toward an open journal lying on the bedside table and pushed up against the lamp, Ruby Blue acknowledges by nodding, then states, "I liked the part in your book where you went to India with college students."

"What?! You were reading my journals?"

What is in those journals? How much did I let loose in that lined and private space? I don't remember. Why have I kept them so long? Chagrin. That is what I am feeling. Well, and quietly smiling, remembering my mother's journals that we found in the closet when we were cleaning out her memory-care apartment, after the dementia finally took her. Mom's first journal began with words, something like, "If you have any decency at all, you will stop reading these words right here. They are private thoughts." And did I stop reading? So much for propriety. I probably should have respected her wishes; she tried to do her best in raising me. And, maybe I should burn my own journals very soon.

"Yeah, I'm reading your journals. You never said they were off limits," Ruby Blue's brow furls as her eyes look away, blinking deliberately, pursing her lips, and nodding. Wary.

She said I could. She don't have to jump evil on me.

"Okay, well, I meant the books, but you did ask."

How much formal education does Ruby Blue have? I wonder. She is curious and smart. But does she have the kinds of critical thinking skills I used to teach? She is suspicious of government and skeptical about science. But then, why do I trust things like expert knowledge and what I think of as basic facts? Perhaps it is because "my people" were the creators and inventers. Is this another kind of privilege or another kind of prejudice?

More to ponder here. Fred understood the power of native ways of knowing, the wisdom of the Native Americans he worked with. He was comfortable in multiple worlds.

"I imagined sitting on that rickety train with you, chugging real slow, with lots of curry smells and coal smoke comin' in the wide-open windows. How long were you on that train with all those people?"

Zoe, recalling, "20 hours."

"Wow. And your friend's brother gets to go anywhere, and people feed him and let him sleep in their houses just because he tells stories? And he isn't called homeless?"

"Yep. Brahmin," Zoe explains. "He and his sister are from the highest caste in Hinduism. Priests and people responsible for teaching and keeping sacred knowledge are part of this group, or caste. I knew the sister in the U.S. where she was not revered, and even looked down on by too many people. Made me angry. Frustrated. But when we got to India, people knew, just by being around her, that she was Brahmin. The transformation was stunning. On the other hand, the strict caste system was difficult for me with some people being 'untouchables' who picked up our used dinner plates and did the cleaning. We were not allowed to do those things. So, both good and maybe less good."

"Let's put travel to India on my vision board!" Ruby Blue smiles sideways, putting one finger on Zoe's knee as they sit together on the bed.

Feeling the intimacy of the touch and winking back, "I like it, for when you are very old, like me, and will be a keeper of sacred wisdom and knowledge. I actually do believe that will happen, Ruby Blue. You have 'the vibe,' as you would tell me."

"You teasin'?"

"No, I truly am not. You are teaching me so much already, Ruby Blue."

"And the students you had with you staying at the orphanage in India. They were afraid of lizards fallin' into their hair? I get that big time. Imagine a lizard creepin' around in my locks. Yeah, that'd be so extra, you dig?"

Ruby Blue moves her hairband down to her neck, runs her hands down both sides of her face, pushing her hair back behind her ears, repositioning the band, and probably unnervingly imagining ensnared lizards.

"Uh-huh," Zoe remembers. "Two of the students pretty much missed the trip those two weeks because they were afraid to leave their little apartment. It was sad. I was the frowny teacher. Maybe I should have gotten hats for them, but we finally decided to just leave them in the dark apartment while we went off to talk with people and visit shrines and temples and lots of magical things.

"I'll never forget the noises—an absolute din of vehicle horns. And the dramatic colors of the women's saris. Women standing in the dust along the side of the road, wearing glowing green and fire-engine red and teal blue saris. Like emeralds. And rubies!"

"And what happened to the little girl you wrote about in your journal?"

"Vikisita? Yes, she thought I was going to adopt her. Every morning when I awoke, even before light, she would be kneeling next to my bed looking directly at my face, kind of like I do to you in the mornings. I would open my eyes and there she would be, all smiles. She was a morning person too!"

Yes, Vikisita. We about broke each other's hearts. I guess even then, I was looking for the child I had lost. Have I been searching for that child I released for all the rest of my life? Perhaps.

"Vikisita went everywhere with me except on the tour bus. We were living at that orphanage the whole two weeks. She would hold my hand. We just hung out, holding hands and smiling; she was like iron filings clinging to the magnet of me. She did not speak English, but I knew what she wanted. I even asked about adopting her but was told that the orphanage director decided who could be adopted. Vikisita wasn't on the list and the director showed me why. As we sat under an auspicious tree in the yard one day, she took the seven-year-old child on her lap and pulled up her shirt, showing that her whole back was covered with raised welts."

Zoe takes a deep breath, pauses, and shakes her head. "Vikisita had been whipped again and again. It was her father who was whipping her and finally a neighbor decided to save the child. She stole her in the night and took her away to the orphanage, never telling anyone.

"Vikisita's back looked like the horrific photos of slaves' scarred backs, people who have been thrashed. The girl's father was an electrician, I was told, so whipped her with electrical wire.

"I knew I could not adopt her and finally had someone tell her that. She cried and cried, but still walked around holding my hand, tears making marks through the dust tarnishing her young face. I wanted to give her something to remember our connection."

"Like what? A gold necklace? Indian women wear them," Ruby Blue says.

"I was told that anything of monetary value I gave her would be stolen and she could be hurt in the process. We settled on giving her a book bag, just like the ones the other, older children had. The last morning, as we left on the bus, I saw her sitting on a porch, bare feet in the dust, her head in one hand, trying to wave with her other hand, while crying. It was painful for everyone."

"I wonder where she is now," Ruby Blue says, partly murmuring to herself, but immediately flashing back to girlhood experiences she had in that house that smelled of poverty, the one with the dark red velvet picture. Silvery letters reading 'God Bless Our Home'. And, next door, the 'Icy Lady' who sold frozen Kool-Aid in Dixie cups from her porch. Where did these memories suddenly come from? And then a memory of being whipped as a tiny girl.

> *They'd send me out to pick out my own switch for my ass-whoopin's. Green, thin ones are the worse. Immature and flexible. Good for the hitter. Bad for me. Brown switches could be dry and hard, so breakable. Temporarily good for me, but maybe bad if the hitter wanted another one when it would break halfway through. So, a blend. Just enough green; just enough brown.*

> *But then they found somethin' better than a switch. Better for them. It was The Belt, readily available in the closet. It was the weapon of choice for its convenience.*

Zoe continues, "A year later, I tried to find out, but they told me there were no records from the orphanage for the children who did not speak English. They were lower caste. She was just one of hundreds of kids who moved on."

"That's messed up."

Then, again pensively fingering her hair with clear concern, "If a lizard fell in my locks, I'd go crazy too. Right now, my naps is free. With this Covid, the only fresh cut I got was from one of the people I lived with 'cause the beauty shops all close."

"Your hair is pretty, Ruby Blue," Zoe says, honestly.

"Don't touch it, though. People seem to think they have the right to touch my hair. I've had store clerks and servers in restaurants touch my hair, like I'm a dog. That is never okay;

they didn't get my permission. It is an invasion, like what that Dr. Foster was doing. Do you know why touchin' my hair is such a major deal?"

Zoe shakes her head, paying full attention to what she is being taught, realizing she is learning things she has never been required to know.

"Slavery roots. That is why. Bet you didn't know that. Our Black bodies were not our own when we were slaves. We were, like, property. We belonged to someone. Imagine what that would feel like. I wonder how Vikisita felt when she learned she wasn't goin' to be whipped anymore. Was she still afraid every night that her daddy would find her?" Then, rhetorically, "Did he ever look for her or didn't he care?"

"I have long hoped Vikisita is safe, somewhere in this world," Zoe murmurs, fingering the ragged journal that had traveled many miles through Andhra Pradesh with her.

Still focused on lizards in her locks, Ruby Blue returns to the topic of hair. "I love talking about hair. You have blow hair—hair that blows in the wind. Behavin' hair. I know more about your hair than you do about mine because your hair is everywhere, in commercials and such. It is called 'good hair.' Not me. You ever see a hot comb? You ever had those burnin' chemicals slathered on your hair and peel off your scalp?"

Pushing her hair behind her right ear, Zoe says, "Like a perm in the old days? Maybe I do know a little. Funny that Blacks pull toward having straight hair and some whites pull toward having curls. It is like tanning. Some White people try to make their skin darker, while some Black people try to lighten their skin, like your story about coffee and chocolate creating a darker baby."

"I'm good with my natural hair movement now. I no longer get my edges laid. My locks need to be free to do what they want. Marcus got peroxide in his hair; looks good on him. But then so does everything."

Zoe smiles, "This is actually funny. My hair looks like a pile of straw these days, sort of mixed white and blond. Not good hair. I cut it myself during Covid. Poor job! But it is me and who sees me? Well, who saw me before you came here? Nobody. All alone all the time. And, I will never, never touch your hair without your permission, Ruby Blue."

The respect is sincere and Ruby Blue nods, acknowledging the honesty. Then a slight chuckle. "Okay, so do you wanna hear a funny story? It's about those damn perms! There was one time I was gettin' a perm done by my mama and cousin. Each of 'em was workin' on one side of my head. All was well until that shit started to burn. My cousin had started the perm before my mama, but didn't wanna take it out early with her DUMB ASS!"

Ruby Blue continues to reminisce, rolling her eyes and shaking her head, "So, half my scalp was on fire while my mama finished up putting chemicals on the other side. I was too young to know it wasn't supposed to burn like that and as a result, the left side of my head was scabbed up for about a week."

Commiserating, Zoe smiles and shakes her head, then stands to leave the bedroom. The women's eyes meet. With gentleness.

ZOE REFLECTION

Spending time with Vikisita took me back to having given up a child for adoption. Did my son end up in an orphanage? Did someone abuse him? Likely not, but you never know for sure. A good home with other kids, I hope. I named him, but am sure someone changed it. I talked with one acquaintance about my effort to adopt Vikisita but he told me I was too old, at age 50, to consider something like that. I think he was a little horrified that I would even ponder doing it. Why?

WE NEED A CHANGE

I t happened on the day of the appointment to visit Dr. Foster in person. Protesters were in the streets near the obstetrics clinic. Black Lives Matter protesters. Both women knew this doctor visit was critically important.

"Get in the car, Ruby Blue. We are going to the clinic."

"Will it be okay?"

White people always givin' orders like they still own somebody. Shit...it's somethin' I gotta do.

"Yes."

Nearing the clinic, various kinds of chants could be heard from activists carrying signs like: "Rise Up!" "Shut Down White Supremacy!" "Black Lives Matter." "Together we Stand." "How many more?" "Fear Less, Love More." "Lift Ev'ry Voice and Sing." "No justice, no peace!" "There will be a new killing today; it just ain't happen' yet."

There is a second group on the street. Agitators with their mouths full of violence against the activists, people hollering the word that rhymes with trigger.

And then a third group. Rioters. People are breaking windows and stealing; people whose actions are hurting the intended, deliberately peaceful calls for change.

A block from the clinic, Zoe turns into a street where her car is quickly encircled. She admonishes herself,

I should not have turned into their lane but it is the street to the clinic and we must get there.

People surround the car and begin rocking the vehicle that is now blocking their pathway.

Furious, Zoe pushes the door open and literally grabs the nearest activist by his collar, pulling him down to where she can be heard. Was he thinking, "Little Old White Woman?" Was he thinking, "Tough Old Bird?" Did not matter.

Ruby Blue thinks to herself,

Oh, wow, okay, White lady. I see you...you must really care. She sorta puttin' herself and her safety on the line for me right now. Maybe it's time to stop givin' her such a hard time...for my baby girl, at least.

The activist Zoe holds onto is big, thick. He is a foot taller than she is. A gray military-style jacket with epaulets covers most of his black hoodie and he walks with determination in his shoulders. He is probably 50 years old.

Holding his gloved wrist firmly and looking up into his face, Zoe declares, "You are going to help me take this woman to the medical clinic one block back. Now."

Probably surprised at her fierce determination, he turns to her as nearby enthusiastic activists continue rocking the car, more in exuberance than in annoyance. In that moment, Zoe is not as invisible as she has come to feel being an olding woman.

"Get some others to help and we'll form a circle around this young woman," Zoe demands.

The activist agrees and motions to several others to join him. Ruby Blue steps resolutely out of the car. She is alarmed but it isn't fear of the activists surrounding them. She is more concerned for Zoe in this larger situation, apprehensive that she is out of her element. Much like how Zoe is concerned about Ruby Blue and her lack of experience with pregnancy scenarios.

Later, the women would discuss how much both of them wished they could have joined the marchers. But not in that moment.

Voice quivering, Zoe again commands, "Form a circle around her and me and help us walk to that medical clinic. Please. It's about a block back."

The man hands off his "We Need A Change" poster to a friend and does as he is asked. It isn't because it is a White woman telling him what to do. It isn't only because it is clear Ruby Blue is a pregnant Black woman needing some help. More like RAW humanity. Change did need to come and it was starting here, now, with this compassionate action.

A group of men and women encircle Ruby Blue and Zoe, whose arms are entwined. Someone steps on Zoe's heel. There is protest turbulence: words floating in the air, music and sirens from somewhere, smoke, and the acidic scent of distant tear gas. Add in odors of perspiration and leathery musk cologne. Zoe thinks she is supporting Ruby Blue. Ruby Blue thinks she is protecting Zoe. Either way, they are getting through this together.

The lead activist, behind his dark glasses and intensity, is in charge in these moments as the small group walks back to the medical clinic, bucking against the surging crowd, which parts. It has to be done.

The activist pounds on the locked clinic door. Staff inside are cowering. But he knocks again, this time gesturing toward the women. With Covid regulations, Zoe should not be allowed to enter with Ruby Blue. But this is different. Everyone nearby is now helping the women, unequivocally demanding they be taken in to the clinic. Activists stand in a protective half-circle until the clinic door opens. The outside noise and odors dim as the door closes behind them. Zoe looks back at the circle of support, giving a masked nod. Humanity has returned.

The nurse at the door has a wispy nest of hair pinned up in the shape of a question mark. Speaking rapidly, she asks, "Are you having headaches or coughing, fever…" The Covid refrain comes.

Both women are quickly ushered into the doctor's examination room, together.

Ruby Blue is shaking. Zoe is shaking. It has been an intense twenty minutes. Zoe thinks, in passing, that her car might well be a target for the rioters at the moment. But that is not the immediate problem they face.

"Your blood pressure is 140/90, Ruby Blue. And yours, Zoe, is 130/80. What a pair you are! Ruby Blue, after you urinate in this cup—clean catch, the instructions are posted on the bathroom wall—put on this gown and lie on that table. Breathe deeply, slowly. Try to relax."

The women exchange sly smiles about the echo of Zoe's refrain on deep breathing and relaxation.

The nurse offers, "We know that even coming to the doctor's office can raise blood pressure and you two came with an escort this time, a riot, so that is yet another factor."

"Protest, not riot." Ruby Blue corrects the nurse, who looks at her full-face, then seeing Ruby Blue's intensive stare, shows a smile that goes no deeper than her lips as she turns away.

* * *

The pair is left alone in the office, waiting for Dr. Foster.

"You straight, ol' lady?"

"You know, Ruby Blue, this isn't my first protest event. What about you?"

"Not mine either but just catchin' my breath right now. I would have given anything to be able to stand and march with them." Ruby Blue remembers.

> *The day will come. My time'll come. Just like when this young man from the community was shot and killed. Shit, the day may come sooner depending on what changes are made. I am rememberin' when Tony Robinson was killed without hesitation by Officer Kenny, just when Tony needed help the most.*

"My first protest was when I was in middle school, right after Tony Robinson was murdered," Ruby Blue states.

"It was a walk-out in front of East High School, held by young people from each of the Madison schools. I remember being so inspired by the older kids around me; to have to fight for justice for this young man. We marched on East Washington all the way to the Capitol. We shut down the whole downtown area. That's when I knew I wanted to be an activist, even if it was just in a small way like that protest. That's why I am just sick I can't join those protesters out there. My people been fightin' for our rights for YEARS NOW!!! But honestly, changes need to be more than just protesting and rioting. Systemic change. That is like changin' the police and changin' the courts and..."

Zoe raises a hand and lowers it, slowly slicing through the air, unambiguously breaking into Ruby Blue's increasingly agitated thoughts and words.

Ruby Blue frowns, thinking,

> *You ain't even listening to me! This is why change can't come because of people's unwillingness to acknowledge that there are problems—and their unwillingness to even hear.*

Interrupting, "You are right, Ruby Blue, but just rest for a few minutes now. Let's see, I'll chatter on while you lie back. Calm. Okay?"

Ruby Blue rolls her eyes but obeys the request. She clearly shows discomfort with what she feels is oppression from Zoe, who continues chattering—blathering on, Ruby Blue feels—about an ICE raid and completely ignoring Ruby Blue's reaction.

"I took a group of students to march against an ICE raid. Immigration and Customs had sent 900 agents who arrested around 400 people without warning, mostly undocumented Mexican nationals working at a kosher slaughterhouse. Children came home to no parents that day, maybe just Granny or Grampy, if lucky. Local churches rallied, taking in the families left behind. Fed them. Tried to get information. Where had the adults been taken?

"We marched through the streets of this rural town as the press recorded the protest. Police lined our route and pro-ICE counter-protesters stood along the sidewalks, shouting things at us in words I won't repeat."

Ruby Blue nods. "Respect."

And what does this have to do with the question you asked me about MY experiences protesting? See, just like a White lady. Making it all about you. I try to let you in and you keep giving me reasons to shut you out.

Zoe puts her fingers to her lips, pensive. Remembering.

Ruby Blue, listening to the now-faint sounds of the protest, is remembering as well, thinking back to Tony Robinson being shot, while half listening to Zoe's story.

Zoe continues talking and hopes she is helping Ruby Blue relax.

"Come to think about it, there was another protest. A Take Back the Night rally. Women, and some supportive men, walked through the late-night city streets, holding candles. Other men stood along the sidewalks, jeering.

"In both situations, there was no way to know what was going to happen. I admire the courage these protesters have today. But they don't know I admire their courage and looking at me, all White and wrinkled, they might stereotypically think I am not supportive. They could as easily have pushed me aside as helped us today when I got out of the rocking car. They did not and I'm glad for both of our sakes, and for theirs."

"Realness recognizes realness," Ruby Blue says, still slightly irritated, as if Zoe should know that this is common sense.

"I'm feeling a little better. You can keep talkin', Zoe." Ruby Blue takes a deep breath and adjusts to a more comfortable position, turning towards Zoe.

Zoe remembers, "The biggest protest I ever saw was in China in 1989. I was just a spectator for what the government subsequently called *The June Fourth Incident*. I had been in China for three weeks studying as a part of my doctoral program. Fifteen of us traveled from Shanghai to Xi'an to Beijing. In every city, there were protests. Thousands of people. It was part of the Chinese democracy movement, and we were seen as representatives of democracy because of our color and our *Americanness*.

"We were greeted by loud cheers and people flashing "V" signs at us—V for victory. For whatever reason, and maybe because we were seen as supportive, I was not initially feeling afraid. In the tightly jammed crowds, people held ropes around their family or friend groups to keep them snuggled together. That is where I got the idea today to have the protesters surround us."

"That big guy today was dope, mighty fine," Ruby Blue says admiringly with her best one-sided smile. "That will be my Marcus in thirty years!"

"Yes, he was intrepid," Zoe smirks, then continues her monologue.

"On June 3rd, we were on a night train headed for Beijing. Once there, we heard distant gun fire outside our safe compound. We did not know that hundreds, maybe thousands, of people were killed that June 4, in Beijing's Tiananmen Square.

"Next day, we were bussed to the airport for emergency evacuation. Where we had seen thousands marching during the previous weeks, now there was only a smattering of people. Beijing was silent, like the Covid streets are these days. We saw burned-out tanks and vehicles, abandoned at the intersections."

Turning to see how Ruby Blue is doing, Zoe asks, "Are you still feeling okay?"

"Yes, I am. Please continue with your story."

Zoe says with compassion, "Okay, good." Zoe places her, now-warm hand on Ruby Blue's shoulder and keeps it there.

She continues, "The airport was jammed, like the street was here today. People had their belongings and even their pets with them. Shoulder-to-shoulder massive chaos. One member of our group—a U.S. military woman—got plane tickets for all of us in a back-room transaction. On the tarmac, three lines of 550 people each, snaking toward three 747 jets. JAL. Japanese Airlines.

"I remember the intensity of climbing into the jet. A friendly, attentive, crisp flight attendant came up, smiled, and used the silver tongs she was holding to pass out rolled, hot towels. Rather than wiping my hands, I used the towel to cover my face. Only then, only then did the tears come. Tears of relief as we headed for the safety of Tokyo."

> *I'm feeling those tears right now. It must be the similarities of what Ruby Blue and I have just gone through with the compassion we experienced, the ongoing struggles of the BLM protesters night after night showing on TV, trying to make people listen and then being undermined by the violence that detracts from their message.*

"Damn, that's some real shit..." Ruby Blue is lying on her left side, her arm circling her belly. "Baby is all fussed up, kickin' up her heels."

"Yes, she is reading your concern, I suppose. Or, maybe she didn't like my stories," Zoe grins. "Let's focus on getting you calm. Enough with the yarns already! We will see if Dr. Foster will let me stay with you for this exam if you are okay with that? We have already violated so many Covid rules, what's one more? At least our circle of support out there in the protest was masked."

"Why is this doctor so slow? I know she knows I'm cold in this tiny-ass gown. Pass me my shirt." Ruby Blue throws her hand up with irritation.

"She may be waiting to see if your blood pressure will settle down. Perhaps they are monitoring me too! Yes, what a pair we are." Zoe slowly shakes her head.

* * *

Dr. Foster knocks and then enters the room saying, "How are you feeling? Your blood pressure is lowering now, which is good, Ruby Blue. Your urine is somewhat dark, but our goal is to prolong your gestational period—the time before you give birth to your daughter. We want her to be as mature as possible and able to breathe on her own."

Tenderly running her warm hands over Ruby Blue's legs, Dr. Foster says, "Your ankles are a bit swollen. Edema. Let me know if this pelvic exam hurts you at all."

Putting a white sheet over Ruby Blue's lap, Dr. Foster explains, "Put your legs in these stirrups and try to relax your knees out to the sides."

Ruby Blue squirms, shifting slightly to the side while squeezing Zoe's hand.

Zoe flinches too, remembering being in this insanely vulnerable position for her first pelvic exam, done to assess her own teen pregnancy.

"I will try not to hurt you," Dr. Foster soothes.

Ruby Blue relaxes some. "It hurts a little. My body feels strange; it just doesn't feel the same."

"That's true. You are pregnant with a little girl! Everything feels normal from the exam. I want you to continue staying in bed, drinking lots of water, eating the preeclampsia diet as you are, and talking to me through the MTAP— Covid Maternal Telehealth Access Project—day after tomorrow, say 10am. You two are doing well. The protesters have moved on down the street now, so one of the nurses will walk you to your car."

> *If I woulda met her first, I wouldn't have been afraid of doctors. If I woulda met her first, maybe I woulda realized that Black women can be doctors too.*

"If it is still there!" Zoe thinks back to having left her car in the middle of the street, surrounded by hundreds of people.

"Right. Let us know."

Maybe seeing Ruby Blue being escorted to the clinic is what saved the car. Anyway, it is fine.

* * *

Ruby Blue is visibly exhausted and goes right to her bedroom, holding Zoe's arm as they walk. Before she is asleep, Zoe brings her a letter.

"This letter was in the mailbox. It is from Marcus; stamped '*INDIGENT*' and '*This letter was mailed from a correctional facility.*' Subtle." Even in her exhaustion, Ruby Blue eagerly reads his words.

> Hey Baby Girl, how you doin'? Our seed? I can't believe that this is how things turned out. It keeps me up at night

worrying about you and our baby. The things I promised I meant. I need you to not give up on us. It is rough right now and I know it is hard to believe it can be anything different. But I believe it. I feel it. It seems crazy but I am at peace, it's like I know this had to happen in order for me to be a better man for our family. I am doing all I can to make sure I get home to you and our seed. A guy on my pod was wheeled out today. They say he got that Covid shit. He looked sicked, but these junkies drying out look like real zombies.

It's really scary to look into the eyes of a person who does not have any dignity. Nothing is beneath him. He gets out in two weeks and says he is going to rob a guy who can't talk about it. A drug dealer. Just knowing that someone like him is out there with my wife and daughter. I am going to come through. You watch and see, my lawyer says he gonna try to get me a good deal. You and our daughter be safe, please. I am sorry I let you down. I screwed up. I was just trying to do what I thought was right. I love you Ruby Blue.

I tried to call but they said there is no money on the account.

I was thinking, dreaming of what I imagine old world Africa was like. The lush, rich full range of green everywhere. A painting. Animals more than we need to sustain our people forever. No guns. Could not have been as comfortable as it is today for many. But it had to feel good to be free.

P.S. So I am watching. I seen a mouse. I knew it had been in the cell as I had found things it chewed on. But now that I have seen the intruder, I am up all night. #Nosleep #Zombieland #creepedout #Iseeiteverywherenow #chroniclesoftheblackexperienceinAmerica

Sincerely your Black King

With tears and a slight smile at his silliness, she hands the letter to Zoe, still standing by her bed.

Zoe accepts the invitation and reads Marcus' words.

"He is a good man, not like your guy who left you."

Zoe nods, "True. You sleep now. It's been a big day. Take care of your little seed!"

MARCUS, CONTINUED

Welcome back; glad you decided to stay a while. I knew you couldn't resist me and miss out on the opportunity to hear my story. I just knew you couldn't resist. I just knew it.

I grew up when I met Ruby Blue. Came into my manhood. Oh, my Ruby Blue. Where I was lighthearted, she was serious. Where I was thinking 'bout today, she had the big picture in mind all the time. The future. Getting' ahead. Making something of herself. Ourselves. She filled in my open spaces.

She's smart. Well, and mostly pissed off about how Blacks are treated in this country. All the ways we can't get ahead; all the barriers we face, like a lack of access to real learning, lack of housing, and jobs. She is determined not to accept these insults. She is a fighter.

She knows the game, always on the lookout for the *poverty pimps*—corrupt leaders who do not want Black and Brown people to lose their grievances, because these pimps are making money from the struggle. Always trying to keep our people down and in a never-ending poverty cycle. Who does that?

And then she got pregnant. My baby. Our baby. I knew I needed to step up and be a man. But the damn virus got in our way. The people she was living with abandoned her and took our Covid stimulus money. My ma was gone. We had no family or friends, just each other. I tried to help. We were desperate. Homeless. So, I robbed that pizza place where I had worked. I knew they kept money in the back office drawer. But I forgot about them stupid cameras. I messed up. I would have paid them back. I swear I would.

Why didn't I ask for help. I shoulda asked for help.

It was terrible being taken away in handcuffs. Embarrassing. They hurt my wrists too. Pure mean. Lots of questions thrown at me. *Name?* That's really none of yo business. *Address?* Well, shit, I didn't exactly have one at that time. I was staying with Dawg and then Ruby Blue got in the women's shelter for one night.

I remember how it felt while being booked and having to put on the issued dingy green hospital-like scrubs. I could smell the stench of the former occupant. Did you know that when your shoelaces and belt are taken away, it is demoralizing? You are left shuffling and holding up your pants—well, if you wanted them held up in the first place. I see why guys let their pants sag now; it is a fuck-you action. But that just ain't me because I know what that suggests. 'You sweet, boy. Pull up your pants!'

And then a holding cell with lots of other guys, all Black except one native dude, I'll point out. They took me, handcuffed, to a pod—they called it—with 25 bunk beds and a little drawer for my stuff. I didn't have much because they took my clothes and my necklace and earrings. They gave me a toothbrush and soap to use in the shower area.

Those other guys were sizing me up. Hey, I don't want no static, I'm a lover, not a fighter. But I love Ruby Blue. How should I act? How do I protect myself? Do I need to act mean, or become mean? Do I need to act angry, or become angry? There is one guard for 25 guys. It's a damn good thing I'm big.

Did you know that someone who takes something is not a thief, but a person who stole?

Do you know how it feels to try to sleep on a steel bed frame, with an issued mattress (if you want to call it that)? I sympathize with my ancestors who were packed shoulder-to-shoulder on the ship. Bodies stacked. Death always on the prowl.

Do you know how it feels to wake up stuck to a plastic tarp-like coating, wet with sweat?

Did you know it is gray and cold in jail? Doors slamming all the time. And how many times do I need to stand and be counted?

But hey, I'm here.

I am sitting here in this jail space. It is almost never absolutely quiet. So, there are degrees of as-good-as-its-gonna-get. Right now, I'm tuned into tonight's entertainment; a guy somewhere yelling to some other unknown voice. He was saying, "I don't want anyone else having fun with my life." And then it came to me. When I do certain things, other people get control over me, like now. They get to have fun with my life, even when shit is hard. I don't want nobody having fun with my life but me. Me and my Ruby Blue and our seed.

Man, what I gotta do to get out of this place?

THIS PLACE

I t is quiet while Ruby Blue naps. A time for reflection and regrouping after the morning excitements, or were they traumas? Thinking about Marcus' comments about getting out of the jail, Zoe sits at her computer. The cursor pulses as she considers what it is she wants to learn more about.

> *My old helpers: accessing my teaching tools. YouTube. A TED Talk. Wikipedia. What key words to search? Injustice? Not actually because Marcus did commit a crime. Prison reform? Why the criminal justice system doesn't work – although some would say it works exactly the way it was designed to work. Justice? Bryan Stevenson's book,* Just Mercy, *which was the shared* common read *at the college one year. Incarceration, race, and slavery? Smith. Another Smith. Clint Smith talking about his book,* How the Word is Passed.

Smith wrote, "Before the war, we owned the negroes. If a man had a good negro, he could afford to take care of him: if he was sick, get a doctor. He might even put gold plugs in his teeth. But these convicts: we don't own 'em. One dies, get another."

> *Smith was writing about convict leasing that followed the Civil War. Not exactly relevant to this search. But is it? What are prisoners paid for their work in the jail, or prison? And health care inside is another relevant topic. I've heard that if a prisoner has a toothache, the prison*

dentist just pulls the offending tooth. (What about the Hippocratic Oath, "First do no harm"?) But then, I expect many arrive in prison with pre-existing health conditions. How does the system afford to deal with all of it? Still, I hear that healthcare in prison is so bleak it is hard to imagine it is accidental. I wonder how Marcus' health is. Ruby Blue obviously didn't have money or the motivation (or the trust) to pay for care during this pregnancy. It is that balance among necessities, things like food, housing, or entertainment. And I suppose health care or wellness come in way last for some young, healthy people.

Clicking the mouse further through the quotes and suggested readings or listening or watching options, Zoe pauses, scanning through snippets of facts.

As a country, we specialize in releasing inmates into desperate, hopeless situations...no way of making money...rights stripped away...They end up in the same neighborhood with the same people, on the same corner; the only difference is that they've now served time...

It is so easy to go from topic to topic, following the meandering paths of the Internet. But baking the fish and cooking vegetables await. I'll let Bryan Stevenson give a TED talk while I cook. Imagine, Stevenson right here in my kitchen. How the world has expanded in mostly good ways.

Zoe pivots the computer screen toward the kitchen as she begins cooking. In the TED Talk, Stevenson states, "...I am persuaded that hopelessness is the enemy of justice; that if we allow ourselves to become hopeless, we become part of the problem. I think you're either hopeful, or you're the problem. There's no neutral place. We've been dealing with injustice in so many places for so long. And if you try to dissect why is this still here, it's because people haven't had enough hope and confidence to believe that we can do something better. I think hope is our superpower. Hope is the thing that gets you to stand up, when others say, 'Sit down.' It's the thing that gets you to speak, when others say, 'Be quiet.'"

> *Hope. Have hope that change can happen. I'll play this TED Talk for Ruby Blue later. Hope. I hope Bryan Stevenson runs for president someday. I'd campaign for him. Wise man. A Mandela kind of human being.*

WONDER BREAD

Ruby Blue, dinner."

"Comin'. We havin' fish? Do you have Wonder Bread?"

"No, don't need it. That's because there are no bones in this fish," Zoe defends.

"Right. Well, catch me if I start choking to death."

The women are startled by the phone ringing. It has been silent for so long. Zoe picks up the dingy, yellowed wall phone and hears,

> THIS IS A CALL AT NO COST TO YOU FROM THE COUNTY JAIL. WILL YOU ACCEPT IT? SAY YES OR PRESS 5.

"Yes."

> ALL CALLS, OTHER THAN PROPERLY PLACED ATTORNEY CALLS, MAY BE MONITORED AND RECORDED.

After saying yes, she hurriedly hands the phone to Ruby Blue, who has stood up eagerly.

"Hey, Baby. How ya doing? So good to hear your voice."

"Yours too. Thanks for callin'. It looks like we finally got this to work. I'd like to move our conversation to another lane, but the phone is tied to the wall."

"Really? Well, here too."

"Old school."

Stretching the spiral cord to the kitchen chair, Ruby Blue sits down near her brown place mat while Zoe places their baked fish back in the warm oven.

"We had a day, no lie."

"Go 'head."

"Zoe took me into town to see the doctor and we got into a protest. I wasn't scared though. Maybe Zoe was."

Ruby Blue looks toward Zoe, who is trying not to listen, while listening, both at the same time, but giving no visible response.

"She don't take no shit though. We got out the car and dudes surrounded us. One guy said to me, 'I see you fam.' They walked us, like a block, through the crowd to the doctor's office. I think I was protectin' her. We heard gunfire in the distance, maybe just rubber bullets. But a stray bullet has no name."

Marcus offers, "You know, death is a way of life in the hood. They fire guns to celebrate some holidays, grieve the dead, as a warnin' or to intimidate. I wonder which one this was? And who was doin' the shootin'? Now you good? Zoe in yo corner for sure."

"Yeah. She is. How you doin'? You gettin' enough food? We havin' fish and maybe Wonder Bread."

"One guy here said it was only fear of jail food that kept him on the straight 'n narrow for years. Then he fell. Now he's a big oily guy. It's that bad, bad fat. That saggin' and droopin' look. He works a jail job only to get the money to purchase as many soda pops, summer sausage, and honey buns as he can. Literally. Just those three things in the canteen bag. Like ten summer sausages—the 8-ounce kind, about six R.C. Cola's, and about six honey buns at a time. That's all he eats and drinks night and day. He say he eatin' himself to death and is gonna make the state pay to care for him until he's dead."

"Funny but not funny. You being the best version of yourself, though, right??"

"Doin' my best. A guy taught me that everyone inside is showin' their weaknesses by what they have or want. Does dude have yoga books? Books on Islam? Photos of his loves? Each one is his weak place. His vulnerability. Easy to bully 'em knowing this and they put it right out there. With big oily dude, attack his food supply and he could crumble, or fight. Yo got—"

ALL CALLS, OTHER THAN PROPERLY PLACED ATTORNEY CALLS, MAY BE MONITORED AND RECORDED.

"Am I your weakness?" Ruby Blue twists the spiral phone cord as she asks this question, a bit shy, but also confident.

She can feel the smile on Marcus' face as he replies, "Oh, yeah. No photos of you by my bunk for sure. I keep us on the D-L."

"Please be careful, I am worried."

"Yeah, I know, me too."

"Be strong, I'm nervous for you, but I know you got this."

YOU HAVE ONE MINUTE REMAINING.

After a pause, Ruby Blue whispers, "We good. My soul ain't no ways tired. Things are gonna get better. We have hope."

"I know. I know. Gotta go, Baby. Love you and our seed."

"Love you, Baby."

* * *

Ruby Blue looks down as Zoe gently takes the phone from her, untwists the cord, and hangs the phone back on the wall. Silence grows in the kitchen as Ruby Blue puts both elbows on the table, shoulders hunching forward, and hands intertwining, holding each other, then rests her chin on her clasped hands, looking pensive.

Zoe places the hot baked fish on her grandmother's old English platter, letting her finger run along the embellished edges as she has done a hundred times before, Then adds green beans, applesauce, and, yes, puts Wonder Bread on the table for them to share. Neither woman mentions the call or the possible Covid exposures they faced during their time in the streets and at the doctor's office.

Zoe has added music—for noise—to their dinner, wondering why she didn't think to do that earlier to give Ruby Blue and Marcus a little privacy. She was not needed for that conversation. After another pause, she tentatively asks,

"What did you think about the protests today?"

"Lots."

Gently prodding, Zoe adds, "More words?"

"I liked the protest signs like: 'We don't need more hashtags.' 'Stop the killing.' 'Killing a *who* is different than killing an *it*.' 'Systemic racism is baked into our system.' 'Racism is its own pandemic.' 'There will be a new killing today; it just ain't happen yet.' "

Nodding, Zoe thinks about Fred's years of work with Native Americans and agriculture. "Sure, all lives do matter. White lives, Red lives, Yellow lives, animal lives, even plant life."

Ruby Blue chews a bite of salmon slowly, reflectively. "True, but not all lives can matter until Black lives do. Not to mention how the Black community has been hurt, lynched, burned, whipped, shunned, shot, whatever, for well over 400 years. That's the difference in my mind. You know, the BLM banner is really one for all decent people to stand under, all who care about equality and oppose racism."

Hesitantly, reflecting some of the angry words from the Internet feeds she had been reading earlier, Zoe adds, "Some say police lives matter too."

Her brow furrowed, Ruby Blue says, "Sure they do, but let's not forget to mention, they haven't been abused in the same ways."

> *Here we go with this shit again. They haven't been terrorized in the same ways Black and Brown bodies have and are continuin' to experience on a daily basis.*

"A career is a choice; a race ain't." Ruby Blue reaches for a slice of Wonder Bread and looks around for butter, sighing as she remembers it is salty and not on the preeclampsia diet.

"How do you compare an occupation to a race? For sure, cops have struggles of their own but that doesn't justify their treatment toward Black and Brown people. I guess what I want to see is respect for basic human—and animal—dignity. Don't plants deserve dignity too? I'm just playin.' But seriously, this stuff is real. There's all kinds of discrimination—like against me as a young, pregnant Black woman. How about the label *welfare queen*? Is that applied to me in some people's minds the minute they look at me?"

A reflective pause and then Ruby Blue playfully offers, "Oh, and thanks for the Wonder Bread. Guess you won't be killin' me off today!"

As she pours more coffee into both their cups, Zoe considers, "Good points. How did the Black Lives Matter movement start? Do you know?"

"BLM started when Trayvon Martin was murdered, I think. I was ten. I remember the community was very upset. Some of them marched but said I was too young to go. My uncle wore a black hoodie and had a Skittles bag taped across his mouth. I won't eat them no mo'—too many associations."

Ruby Blue takes a sip of her coffee. "Remember when I was telling you about that protest I did in middle school?"

"Yes," Zoe nods.

"I remember bein' sad thinking about how that could have been me or someone I was close to."

Ruby Blue pauses and shifts in her chair, trying to hide the pain she is beginning to feel.

"Terrible. This young man being shot multiple times, all over his body...right there in the comfort of his home...his DEAD BODY on the stairs in a pool of blood. For months after the shooting, the blood still remained on the sidewalk and the doorway of his house. I can't even imagine how his mother felt. I would be unraveled if that was my baby girl. Just completely destroyed."

Zoe decides, consciously and even uncharacteristically, not to change the subject as the talk gets more personal and potentially more volatile.

> *I'll take a chance here. I'll ask more questions; this conversation is going deeper than we have previously felt safe enough to explore. Deeper on such important issues and clearly questions Ruby Blue has already considered.*

Zoe offers, "After riots, I've heard people ask, 'Why do *they* burn *their* own neighborhoods?' What do you say about that?"

Holding the fork to her mouth, then hesitating, Ruby Blue rhetorically asks, "Who is *they*? They is poor people. Some say *under-resourced*. You know, we don't own nothin'. I don't have no Granny's shiny chair or platter or sugar bowl, or everything else that is around you here. This table. These chairs. You know the hood wasn't mine to begin with, right? But we had to make it ours. It's not that we don't care. People just need something to smash on hot summer days. Summer isn't a noun for poor people."

"What do you mean?" Zoe asks, honestly, feeling uninformed in light of this wise young woman's lived experience.

"Summer isn't vacation time—go to the lake, be playful. It is work time, if you are lucky enough to have a good job."

"Work. A verb."

"Sure. You asked if I would call a cop if I was in trouble. No. Even if he or she is Black. Not even if I was the "victim." Black police may have things to prove and fewer ways to prove 'em. Or it could be that they are just brainwashed by the black and blue order. The police patrol our streets more than they do here, like an occupyin' force. I haven't seen a single cop car in this neighborhood since I got here, and I've been watchin'. What's equal about that?"

Zoe continues, "I was pulled over for speeding recently, well, before Covid. The officer asked me if I had any illegal substances or guns in the car. I laughed at the question, and so did he. I could tell he was required to ask it, even of an elder driving an old hybrid car ten miles over the speed limit in a 25-mph zone. He gave me a verbal warning. So, do you think there is more crime in poor, and often Black, neighbor-hoods? Could the police just be patrolling there to protect residents? Do too many see Blacks as inherently criminal? I guess what I'm trying to figure out is, what's your perspective about all these things."

"No, I do not think Blacks are inherently criminal; but if we are, it's because of the system. Crime might be higher, but why? Maybe because summer is not a noun. We struggle to make money; to survive. That is what caught Marcus up."

> *Here I am doing what I never thought I'd do. Schoolin'*
> *a White woman about the chronicles of the Black*
> *experience in America. Maybe it is okay; she seems to*
> *honestly care. But what good can come of it?*

Silence seeps into the room. There is tension in the air and Zoe can feel the edge of anger in Ruby Blue's comments, so changes the subject for a minute.

"Be sure to drink that water."

Ruby Blue grimaces, "It would be nice if I wouldn't be interrupted every time I was speaking." Then she drinks the water anyway.

Zoe looks down, embarrassed.

Noticing Zoe's chagrin, Ruby Blue offers, "Can I show you this song called *"I Can't Breathe"* by H.E.R, this might better describe what I'm tryin' to say."

After listening to the song, Zoe reaches back into the space that is cooling again, after having warmed up slightly, but not near a boiling point. She asks, "So, what would you do to change the police? Defund them? That has been the call this year. What does that mean to you?"

Annoyed, Ruby Blue explains, "Don't it seem like cops serve you but police me; call my people super-predators, but yours victims; call my people crack addicts, but call yours people-struggling-with-addiction; call me the N word, but call you ma'am? But most importantly, when you see a cop, do you see a weapon or a badge? Depends on your life experience and, probably, your color, don't it. Like H.E.R. said, you're trying to tell me that the protector and the killer are in the same uniform—"

Now, deflecting again, and interrupting Ruby Blue's building anger and stress.

"Okay, another story, Ruby Blue, while you finish that fish before it gets too cold."

Zoe recalls, "I was in The Arch in St. Louis once. There were truly creepy little elevators that climbed to the top, all rough and jerky and rickety-feeling. About six, as I remember, people to a car, facing each other and sitting knee to knee. There I was, just looking at the view, and this stranger started serenading me. Loudly. People probably thought we were together. I kept moving away from him. He followed, singing a sensual, suggestive song. I decided to leave and he was positioning to ride in the same elevator car. I found the cop among the forty or so visitors and asked him for help. Without question, he got in the same car with me, rode down, and then waited while I escaped the 'predator' who was still up top, maybe singing to a new victim. I don't know what happened to the predator."

Why does she call 'em a predator? What does predator mean to her? There was that six-year-old girl riding in a car with me once when a cop passed us. She

screamed, "Ruby, he is coming to get us!" Such deep
fear. So early. Who is the real predator?

Ruby Blue ponders, chewing slowly, then asks, "You were saved by the cop. Just one question. If it had been me, would he have thought I did something to cause the incident? Maybe. Maybe not. I try not to be paranoid. But we can't know, which is a main part of the problem. I want cops to intervene like the cop did for you. But I also want them to stop usin' excessive force and shootin' innocent Black and Brown kids. We have enough hashtags. We don't need more balloons with names on them. Parents shouldn't have to keep puttin' flowers at intersections or continue makin' T-shirts with the endless list of names."

"That's tragic and not the type of policing I would support. What do you think needs to be done to stop this from happening in the future?" Zoe questions.

"I don't know exactly," Ruby Blue considers, looking around for some butter then remembering their salt restriction, again.

"I do know that not all cops are bad. So, how do we know the difference? Do some shoot because they are afraid? If I was facing someone with a gun, what would I do? Shoot first and ask questions later, or would I talk to the person? Try to reason. Find common ground, like, 'Hey, we all from the same neck of the woods so let's talk this through and no one gets hurt.' Maybe that is naïve."

Ruby Blue reaches for another slice of the Wonder Bread. "I don't know. We seem to be a progressively more violent society. I heard that President Obama, a Black man, was the best gun salesman in America because handgun sales sky-rocketed during his two terms in office. Fear? Of what?"

Quiet fills the room as Ruby Blue pauses. The only sound is the clink of Zoe's fork on her China plate. She reaches for a slice of Wonder Bread too.

Zoe offers, "Defunding police could mean adding more human service workers…"

Ruby Blue interrupts and adds, "Quite frankly, I'm not too convinced the police should be asked to deal with homelessness, drug addiction, mental illness, domestic violence, or poverty. Doesn't it set them up for failure?

"I think the people we should be calling are mental health providers or social workers. Someone who is more used to doing this work—to deescalate the problem—not resort to violence."

Ruby Blue thinks to herself about the young man, Tony, who was killed by the police.

> *Tony was struggling with his own demons but that doesn't mean he deserved to have seven bullets in his body. How many people from the community are still haunted by that killing. Still angry. Still fearful. Still sad.*
>
> *How many people from the U.S. are still haunted by the numerous other killings, like Michael Brown, Eric Garner, George Floyd, Breonna Taylor, Philando Castile, Daunte Wright, and another name, and another name, and another name.*
>
> *New names are constantly being added to the list that never ends. The impacts of these killings just don't leave us. They are forever reminders; the nightmares we can never forget.*

There is always one murder that sticks with each of us personally.

Tony was mine.

Ruby Blue exclaims, gesturing with her butterless Wonder Bread to make the point, "Think about wellness checks. How many Black and Brown people have we lost to a mis-reading of the situation? Blacks are killed by the police three times more often than Whites. It's payin' attention to details like this that would help the Black community have fewer trust issues. It would also help if the police weren't always ready to pull the trigger before takin' time to engage with us."

Zoe adds to Ruby Blue's thoughts, "Do you know what 'implicit bias' is, Ruby Blue? I don't mean to sound like a know-it-all. The term was written on one of the protest signs I saw and it reminded me of the book I read called *Biased*. Intuitive, like in the blink of an eye. Maybe that is part of it. Like you said, you'd try to work with the person. Your first assumption would be that you had things in common, right, as humans."

"Exactly," Ruby Blue nods, wiping up the last of the herbs from the salmon with her bread. She adds, "So, as I understand this, implicit bias is where our minds go in a split second. Before we think about something. It comes from our life experiences and assumptions. Maybe it is a survival skill because we don't always have time to figure things out. Sometimes we just act."

The women pause, taking time to reflect. Then Ruby Blue offers,

"Implicit bias. Like White men can't jump, or Asians are good at math, or Black people are lazy. Are there implicit biases for all groups of people? People assumin' I am wanting welfare because I've got no money, so got myself pregnant—which is pretty hard to do, I'll point out." Ruby Blue snickers. "It takes two."

Zoe stands up. Stretches her shoulders and arms. "Good points. I want to talk more later. Thank you for helping me understand beyond my book-learning. Want to take a cookie to bed with you?"

"No, I'm good. I wonder how remnants of the slavery laws and Jim Crow caste rules impact me today. Were they similar to the barriers from these Covid restrictions? Implicit bias—"

"G'd night, Ruby Blue. I'm too tired. Thanks for today."

As she puts the dinner dishes next to the sink, "Night, Zoe. Me too. Oh, and is it okay if I write in one of the blank journals in your office, in my room? And, also let's check on more money for Marcus to call me again. That was great, but too short. I promise to pay you back, one day."

* * *

Zoe elects to stay awake knowing it is too early for her to go to bed because she won't sleep through the night. She decides to wash the dinner dishes by hand. There has always been something soothing for her with hands in hot, soapy water. Something cleansing of more than dishes. The mind? Maybe the soul? She hums quietly over the sudsy dishes. Didn't Thich Nhat Hanh say something like, *When you are washing the dishes, be washing the dishes?* One thing at a time. Be in the moment.

And yet her mind meanders slowly, wearily away from the water's warmth to thoughts of preeclampsia, the protests, the dinner conversation, and the students she had taught over the years. Literature. Story. How do they differ from lived experience? There is passion and wisdom in Ruby Blue's words and thoughts. What will be in her future? How can she, Marcus, and the baby thrive in a world that too often discounts what they say? What they tell? What they ask for? And now, with a probable felony on his record, how will Marcus reenter the world? Housing? A job? School? Will people take a chance on him? Trust him?

Zoe sits, sinking into her favorite and worn chair. She watches the orange-flecked glow to the west indicating where the sun has set, something she already knows. So much to ponder.

Avoid talk disguised as action, she tells herself. What do they say? *Try again. Fail again. Fail better. Or, more explicitly, act and talk and learn and fuck up and learn some more and act again and do better.*

Yep, many right ways to say the same thing.

JUSTICE FOR ALL

Ruby Blue goes to her room, but continues to be troubled by the day's events and the conversation with Zoe. One of the protest signs haunts her.

There will be a new killing today; it just ain't happen yet.

So often we write more than we consciously know. This was one of those times as she picks up a blank journal. She writes about how many Black men have been killed by police brutality.

She mouths these words in silence, thinking of all the Black and Brown people who have died from police bullets. She writes through her anger. Fast. Cathartic. A spoken-word piece.

Justice for all

When the sun goes down and the pigs come out, shooting from all directions, did you know they're trying to kill our whole generation.

They shoulda listened to our cries or maybe they should have listened to Eric's cries when he couldn't breathe (gasp) gasping for air, barely taking that last breath, he must have had a fetish for watching the light leave that lifeless black body, they always ask for forgiveness but like his wife said, (quote) "No, I won't accept his apology, no I won't

142

accept his condolences. He's still working, still getting his pay check, still feeding his kids and my husband is six feet under."

Six shots to an innocent body. That ain't no way to die. Left him to rot. Four hours they left Mike's body to be admired by all the other pigs that come out after dark.

There will be a new killing today; it just ain't happen yet.

Emmett Till just got killed but all he did was whistle, the white man strikes again, destroyed such a beautiful picture, she couldn't even recognize his features, the only reason she knew it was him was because of his daddy's ring that somehow stayed on his finger.

There will be a new killing today; it just ain't happen yet.

We need to stand up and fight for justice for all.

But wait I almost forgot, what about Trayvon Martin, I thought his life was priceless, but somehow that Arizona Tea and the taste of the rainbow gave the signal, only his killer should have known that just because you wear a hood doesn't always mean you from the hood.

Three questions:

One, since when did you have the right to take away my life?

Two, since when was my life worth any less because you don't like the color of my skin?

Three, did you ever think maybe I like the skin I'm in?

There will be a new killing today, it just ain't happen yet.

Gone too soon.

Precious souls lost.

We will never forget.

Ruby Blue gives herself the space to let the events go for the moment.

She lets them bleed onto the paper as the never-ending cycle healing process begins again.

THE TALK

Morning, morning, Ruby Blue! I made those waffles you like for our breakfast. Here is the coffee. We meet with Dr. Foster at ten this morning through the Telehealth system. Before that, do you want to take a relaxing bath? Tub full of warm water and you just rest there? Sound good?"

"Yes. My skin is getting ashy."

"What does that mean?"

Wringing her hands together, Ruby Blue explains, "My skin dries out without lotions. It isn't as noticeable on White skin, I don't think, but on Black, my skin looks like ashes. My uncle used to joke that our family kept Jergens in business. My Granny used to say to rub cocoa butter into our skin, especially in the hidden spots behind ankles and around knees. If I can reach them over my stomach! Care for my body. That is a human right, right?"

"I'll see what I have. A light sesame seed oil for sure."

Looking into her coffee cup, Ruby Blue muses, "Your skin is not a color, is it? Really, more like an absence of color. Maybe silvery. Maybe pinkish like a summer fruit. It seems to pick up the colors of the clothes you are wearing, so more pink when you wear red, like the shirt you have on, and darker when you wear brown. That's what I see. White isn't better; just different. For all of us, skin just separates our insides from our outsides."

Smiling at this opinion, so early in the morning and considering, then rejecting teasing Ruby Blue about becoming a morning person, Zoe adds, "I agree. If I were any paler, I'd be clear like a salamander that has spent her life in a cave, without sunlight. As I look at the veins on my hands now, in old age, I actually am getting to be clear, or blue."

Nodding, "There are jokes we make about Black skin. So dark you could go naked to a funeral. Don't stand in front of an old school chalkboard 'cause you'll disappear."

"That's cruel, isn't it, Ruby Blue?"

Zoe turns on the radio news and the women eat in silence for a few minutes, waking up slowly. Ruby Blue rubs the top of her stomach, feeling a new kick from her daughter: that, now routine and more pleasant, snakes-in-the-belly feeling.

Thinking about raising her daughter, Ruby Blue muses, "Black is sometimes seen as evil, white as pure. Like, 'going to the dark side.' Look at those old Western movies where the bad guys wear black hats and the good guys wear white. What am I supposed to think about that? What will I teach my daughter about that? Maybe we just won't watch those movies."

Shaking her head as she continues to think about becoming a mother, "But how can I protect her from other stuff? I suppose Marcus and I will give her 'the talk.' Tell her that the rules are different for her in spite of what the media and all will have promised is open to her. And that, in truth, she will be powerless to do anything about it. Like destiny denied. Or maybe she will grow up in that new post-racial world folks sometimes talk about. But I ain't holdin' my breath."

I'm thinkin' about Granny, before she died, sitting me down that week after Trayvon was shot and givin' me the talk. I did not want to hear what she was sayin' and she did not want to tell me either. But it was essential. It was about survival.

"What do you mean by 'the talk'?" Zoe asks as she adds Karo syrup to her waffle, a favorite of hers and something to substitute for the lack of salty butter—also an all-time favorite. She is glad the syrup was available when she ordered more sweet potatoes.

Looking at the Karo syrup coming sluggishly out of the dark bottle as if it is something foreign, which it is, and wondering if it is as bad as the tea Zoe keeps trying to push for her, Ruby Blue adds, "Black parents teach their kids how to survive in a world that tends to hate them. Out there, they don't love our kids like we do. Lots of parts to 'the talk,' like never turn your back on a cop with a gun. When stopped by an officer, put your hands on the dash. Head down. Don't argue. Be *compliant*. Never move or reach for anything. Expect to be followed in stores. Never touch unless you are ready to buy and keep your hands in sight at all times. Never give your child a toy gun and do not allow them to play with anyone else's gun outdoors."

Ruby Blue raises her voice as she recites the rules she has been taught. "Expect to be checked if you don't have a receipt for things you purchase. Expect to be the last one served and acknowledged when in establishments. You catch my drift? See the pattern. It's always us vs. them, but it be their own people they gotta watch out for."

Zoe nods, remembering, "Some studies show, I've read, that humans recognize people who look like them better than those who don't. I was once with a woman from Nepal who came to the university back when I was a student. I was helping her acclimate and told her she had to go into a certain office to talk with the woman with red hair about the issue she was facing. She went into the office while I waited in the hall, looked around, then came out, saying she did not know what 'red hair' looked like. There was no such thing in Nepal and she could not see what I meant by red hair."

Ruby Blue says, "And I can relate. I remember being in middle school, it was my first time realizing that I was surrounded by mostly White kids. I remember it being tough to keep their names straight because I couldn't recognize the differences in their facial features."

"I had trouble separating my students sometimes too," Zoe smiles, acknowledging her embarrassing truth. They nearly all had long blond hair and blue eyes." A pause, "Do you think you would be White if you could, Ruby Blue?"

Tilting her head thoughtfully, taking the question seriously, knowing it was asked honestly, even if a bit innocently, "Is white a color or a state of mind? I wonder. I guess it is a color."

Ruby Blue thinks,

I would argue it's a state of mind but if you ask society, they'll tell you it's a color.

"No, I wouldn't change a thing, but I'd like more respect for who I am. I love who I am and the skin I'm in. I just wish I wasn't treated as if my life is less valuable than anyone else's. I wish I didn't have to encounter racism on a daily basis."

Ruby Blue raises her fist into the air, thumb resolutely crossing bent fingers, symbolizing Black Power. "But I am me. A Black woman. I am a STRONG Black woman. That will forever be me."

Silently wishing she had melting butter on her waffle while ignoring Ruby Blue's gesture because she does not know what to say about it, Zoe reports, "We had Shirley Cards in our house when I was a little girl; I don't know why. Did you ever hear of them? Kodak used those cards to show correct skin tone balance, it said on the cards. The correct colors and tones and shadows, of course, were for White skin. The original Shirley was a Kodak employee.

"Have you ever noticed how often Black faces disappear in photos? In one of my classes, I would show this film about community activist Saul Alinksy and his battle with the Eastman Kodak Company about them not hiring Blacks. I remember Alinsky being quoted as saying something like, 'Kodak's biggest contribution to race was the invention of color film.' I suppose the camera worked like some human eyes, blotting out darker skin tones."

> *Okay, stop this. I feel like I'm trying to force a discussion about race and that just isn't fair to Ruby Blue; I don't have that right. Obviously, she has thought about —has lived through—these issues. Conversations about race are about real people and real hurt. Then again, is having the conversation worth the risk? I don't know. I do know that my family did not need to have "the talk" with me.*

"Anyway, I'll fill the bathtub and find the body oil for you. And drink water, drink water! Telehealth at ten and then we will see how to put more money on the phone for Marcus."

Ruby Blue smiles, thinking about her dude.

* * *

The women separate, going to their own tasks and thoughts, both increasingly pleased to have company. Someone to share stories and real-life experiences with about more than the mundane of life. Someone who responds in ways the TV news and robo-phone calls aren't offering during this time of isolation and uneasiness as Covid death tolls rise daily, showing up as tallies in the bottom right corner of cable news stations, and social unrest expands.

Zoe puts the oil next to the closed bathroom door. "Here is that oil. Go ahead and use it up if it works for you; we can order more from Amazon."

After being warmly held by the bath water, then spreading the oil on her arms, legs, knees, and face, Ruby Blue wraps Zoe's fleece bathrobe, which she now wears much of the time, around her body and extended belly. Wiping away a circle of fog from the mirror, she studies the eyes that she has been looking out through for these many days. Now safe. Cozy. Warm. She walks back into the kitchen where Zoe is cutting vegetables for later, as usual. Ruby Blue shows Zoe her smooth hand, after having used the oil. They put their hands side by side on the table, seeing that the only differences between them are the color of their skin and number of wrinkles.

We are all one being, just different.

Humans.

Being.

WHAT'S GOIN' ON?

Pleased they have excellent Internet access and remembering how limited it was for Fred and his students on the reservation—so patchy he did not even consider teaching online—Zoe points to the info sheet. "Okay, here is the Telehealth link we need."

She types in the link address and the video call begins.

"Hi, I'm Tatiana. I'll be your nurse today. The records show you have mild preeclampsia. How has your blood pressure been? Stable?"

"130/80, most of the time. We are using Fred's blood pressure cuff."

"Good. We want this to stay steady for you and the baby, your daughter."

"Headaches or changes in vision?"

"Nope."

"What is your weight now?"

Tatiana was a woman of few words or maybe the Telehealth system encouraged this sort of interaction. Just getting to the point because so many people were needing access to health care of any kind.

"We think I have gained about two pounds since I saw Dr. Foster. Where is she?"

"She is helping another patient today. With Covid, you know how stretched we all are, but so very glad we can at least connect via this online system."

"It sounds like you and Zoe are maintaining your diet and weight well. Any new upper abdominal pain?"

Ruby Blue twists in her chair, finding a more comfortable position, "Sometimes the baby kicks a lot."

"Are you on WIC or a basic food stamp program, Ruby? What are your plans for after the baby is born?"

Angrily leaning more closely to the camera on Zoe's monitor, "I don't know yet. We will see. Why are you asking me about food stamps and all?"

"Just trying to help you plan, Ruby. This is a major life change and we want it to go well for you and your daughter."

"My name isn't Ruby. It is Ruby Blue.

Tatiana replies, tensely, "Okay, sorry. In a month or so, we will talk about lactation consultation and other postpartum questions."

"Yeah. Whatever. I want to meet with Dr. Foster next time."

"We will call with the time for your next Telehealth visit, Ruby, uh, I mean Ruby Blue."

Standing up, Ruby Blue heads for her bedroom. Zoe can feel her tension, and humiliation, but, again, doesn't know exactly what to do, so does nothing in the moment as she signs out of the Telehealth website.

Just leave her alone for now.

Zoe flashes to her own memory of giving birth, and shivers.

> *I could see the nurses down the hall, standing together and laughing. It seemed like they were a block away. I tried to call out to them, but they did not look toward me, or seem to hear me. Blood and enema were gushing*

*down my legs. Cold. The cold was knifing in. Every-
thing was so cold. Is this a dream?*

* * *

Two hours later, after putting on a new tablecloth and finding different dishes, just for some variety in the ongoing bleary sameness of Covid life, "Lunch."

"Yeah."

Sitting down, the only words were Marvin Gaye singing "What's Going On," one of Zoe's favorites from back in the day. Only love can conquer hate...Protests from a different time and place.

"I found a book I've had for a very long time and had forgotten about. I was reading it last night. Do you know about the author who edited this book, Toni Morrison? You might be very interested in some of her books."

"I have read *The Bluest Eye*. I ain't stupid," Ruby Blue chirps, still smarting from the nurse's questions and not knowing where to place the hurt, so was attacking the person closest to her, but without conscious malicious intent.

"You are right. I am very sorry. Look how many times we are saying 'sorry' to each other. Maybe this is good, building awareness. Deeper sensitivity. Anyway, this is a compiled book Morrison created and published way back in 1974: *The Black Book*. It is the history of many elements of Black life in America, the good and the bad. She contends that one of the best sources of resistance is remembering. I think it will interest you. See my Post-It note on page 41? Ruby Blue Smith, Bessie Smith's niece. She was a singer. Did you know you have a famous name?"

Ruby Blue looks down at the book resting between them, mildly interested.

Zoe opens to another bookmark. "And I was smiling at the hair oil recipes on page 189, after we were discussing how much you love to talk about hair. Other than the axle grease recipe, my favorite hair oil formula starts with one gallon of 90-proof cologne spirits—stay away from open flames! Add a little lemon, orange, and bergamot. Some vanilla, and shake until well blended. Add 1½ pints of soft water. Imagine the rich smells. I wonder what cologne spirits were, or are? We probably won't make up any of this brew."

"Let me see."

Zoe slides the book across the flowered tablecloth and around the sugar bowl, past the heart-shaped wire napkin holder.

Why does this table look like a pinball machine with all the random obstacles. Are they necessary or are they just relics of my dated family traditions?

Zoe indicates another image, this time on page 9, with her crooked pointer finger.

Interesting that Ruby Blue is looking at the page rather than my arthritic finger. I like that.

"Here. Look at this sickening photo of a man, a slave, who was whipped, repeatedly. His back reminds me of Vikisita's back, the little girl in the orphanage. How do people do things like this to other human beings? I'll never understand."

Ruby Blue drums a finger hard on the book, pointing at an advertisement. "And look at this ad for selling human beings; it says someone could buy '... a 'likely light-skinned girl about 17 or 18 years old'. This is further proof—not that we needed it—of what I was talking about with names. Families sold and separated. Just randomly."

While Zoe is putting the leftovers away, Ruby Blue lays out a page in *The Black Book* for her to look at.

"Look. Here is a reason I can never trust the police. Look at this, here on page 27. Just look. 'Attention Colored People of Boston. Watch out for the police. The mayor has empowered them to be kidnappers and slave-catchers.' My mistrust goes way, way back to 1851 in this case. There is real history in this book. It would take a year to read it, but I'm catchin' pieces even looking through it. My family history. But what would my African heritage be if it hadn't been interrupted by slavery? My heritage did not begin with the Middle Passage."

Zoe, her elbows now resting on the table, peers down at the open book, watching Black hands touch the legacy pages.

Yes, part of her heritage. Marcus' heritage. The baby's heritage. My heritage too. History to remember. But what is missing from this book are the African legacies that preceded, like Ruby Blue was asking about. I am vaguely remembering a Baldwin line from Notes of a Native Son *about the past making the present – what was his word? Understandable? Clear? No, maybe coherent? Geeze, I taught books like Baldwin's but I did not understand them at this level. I knew not I knew not. Ruby Blue is my teacher, but I must not assume she knows all about oppression just because she is Black. And, oddly, Covid and her pregnancy are giving us our opportunity to both teach and learn.*

Placing a glass of water on the table and watching a single drip move down the outside, Zoe reflects aloud, "This is such important information. It tells us more about how we all are as humans and why we feel and see what we do, like me having this old napkin holder and aged tablecloth of daisies and dandelions. I suppose we all have some degree of material legacies we can touch, as well as unexamined implicit biases, like we discussed earlier. But I wonder how many people stop to think about where they may have come from, how they impact their choices, and why they continue to hold them—or believe in them?"

Absently turning to the next page and sipping the water, Ruby Blue slowly nods.

"I'm thinking about the man who helped us get to Dr. Foster's office," Zoe contemplates aloud. "He did not put his life on the line, but he stood up for what he felt was right. Where in his family or his upbringing did that belief come from?"

Ruby Blue continues to turn page after page slowly, looking at the photos and reading some of the text.

> *I wonder exactly what stories and beliefs have been passed on to me through the generations. Through slavery. Maybe strength and determination. Yes, that for sure. What else? I have a memory of an aged man telling me that slaves worked from sun to sun. "Kin to cain't;" can see light to can't see light. Yes, strength and determination. But how else does the history tell me why I am who I am?*

"Hate. Hate and mistrust passed on through generations. You know, when I first heard I was going to live with you overnight, I said, 'I don't do White people and I don't do old people.' I guess that was wrong, wasn't it? Just keepin' it real."

Trusting this woman is a big ask. I'm not just frontin' and putting on a good face. This is for real.

Nodding and still resting her elbows on the table while leaning in even closer to the open book, Zoe adds,

"And me? I was upset that you were so young and pregnant, which goes to my past history too. Much as I fight against it, I sometimes feel awkward around young people., maybe I feel inept or clumsy. Isn't that odd given that I was a teacher."

Zoe pauses, remembering, "When I was young, an older woman was bullying me at work. A gaslighter. She was flaunting the things and experiences she had. I remember thinking to myself, 'You may have power over me now, but I have something you will never have again. Youth.' If I had been more mature, I suppose I could have tried talking with her about what I was feeling. But I wasn't confident enough."

Zoe shakes her head, silently wondering if she has revealed too much, then continues,

"Prejudice is everywhere. I wonder why that must be. People can pass laws, but they don't necessarily change attitudes. You know, an example is calling this Covid "the Chinese virus." That has led to attacks on random Chinese and other Asian people. Pure prejudice. Those people had nothing to do with a virus. They are victims like the rest of us. Cold, icy, thoughtless prejudice."

Nodding, remembering life events she wishes she could put away forever, Ruby Blue sighs. "I have experience with that. I have been treated as 'the help' by Whites, an employee rather than a customer. I have been followed around in stores, all the time, when people assume I'm going to steal something, maybe because they assume I don't have the money to pay. People touching my hair, like we talked about. People who say my name is too hard to pronounce, which is why I have that line, 'Then just call me Ms. Smith.' I get to tell them who I am. But THEY get to forget how they treated me and move on with their lives. I don't."

"Sorry about all of this. Sorry you have had to experience these things," Zoe acknowledges.

Twisting her head to the right, knitting her brows, and raising one hand with a gesture of impatience, her fingers flaring in an explosion-like gesture, Ruby Blue motions, "Want me to go on? So many examples.

"You asked what Marcus and I are going to name our daughter and we had talked about Queenie or Diamond. Funny though 'cause someone—a White woman—asked me, 'Why do Black people give their kids such funny names?' And worse, why did I push my pain down and question our daughter's name based on that comment? Believe what that woman said? Another person asked me if the baby-daddy was in the picture. Damn, that's messed up. Look at the assumptions in that question: I am not married, which I'm not, but that is none of their business. An assumption that he would leave me."

Then pausing, uncomfortably. "Oops, sorry. That was what happened to you, Zoe. And them assumin' I was going to go on welfare to support my daughter, like that Telehealth nurse said. And people wonder why so many African Americans flash anger so quick. My granny used to say, 'White folks kill you if you want too much, kill you if you want too little.'"

A long sigh and deep breath. Zoe offers a hand on Ruby Blue's arm and the women sit in bonding silence.

"I have to go to the bathroom. Again. Maybe after you will tell me about that place you went to when you were pregnant."

Interesting moments here, Ruby Blue, my teacher. Our life experiences are overlapping. In a sense, you are living in a home for an unwed mother, just like I did 1,000 years ago.

Standing up with a weighted effort, Ruby Blue utters, "I don't mean to ask questions that are too personal, and I know people got to reckon with the hand God dealt them, like a dark memory of an auction block we carry within us—a past that is never really past. But there are many ways to reckon."

"No, I promised I'd tell you, Ruby Blue. But first, I'll get you some coffee and a banana."

"When I get back from the bathroom, how about if I lie on the couch in the living room for a while? But you better not forget to tell me about that home; you bad woman. Always changin' the subject."

* * *

The women move to the living room, and draping the old-fashioned yellow and brown crocheted blanket over Ruby Blue's right shoulder and tucking it in around her knees, Zoe asks, "Are you comfy? Do you like that pregnancy pillow?"

"My preg pillow and I are chillin'. It's a blessing that you are finally gonna talk!"

Zoe pulls the antique velvet striped chair closer to the couch, as if she is going to be telling a story at a campfire. Fred had never liked the chair with what he felt was its pretentious country French style. But Zoe knew her grandmother had cherished it and so she did too. Besides, it fit her just right. Her feet touched the ground when she sat in it and that wasn't the case with all furniture. She visualized where the chair had come from, always located in its assigned spot in her grandparents' home, just to the side of the diamond-glass chandelier that looked like glistening, soft rain dripping from the ceiling. So long ago.

She smiles to herself thinking that even her unconscious thoughts are trying to avoid talking about her pregnancy. Changing the subject from The Home to thoughts about her grandparents. But, as promised, she redirects her memory to the family drama she caused, being glad her grandparents had become earth, as Fred would have said, before the dishonor.

THE HOME

Zoe begins, "I learned a lot from being pregnant. I was never a girl again after that. A woman. That may happen for you too, but then you have Marcus, so your situation is dissimilar. I was in a completely different place than my school classmates. It was like I couldn't relate to them any longer, and, of course, my family had hidden my pregnancy, even from my siblings. It was that shameful."

Squirming and trying to get comfortable, Ruby Blue urges, "And? Get to the story."

> *This woman tells stories in circles, just like my uncle used to do. Mistress of redirection. Sometimes he would get so lost in the gravy that we never got to taste the meat.*

"Okay. Okay! The home I was taken to was in San Antonio, Texas. It was another world from where I had grown up. I don't know why my parents chose to take me there, but they did. We never talked about any of this before, during, or after. I hadn't understood all the privileges I had, so some hands-on learning was taking place—like you have experienced.

"The city itself was a learning opportunity. I saw a person being chased and then stabbed on a downtown street. I was living in a Latino—today, a Latinx—community. I remember going to get a haircut one day, in a home-based beauty shop, and the stylists all coming over to touch my hair because it was different, softer, I guess, than most of the hair they usually cut. I felt like you described, Ruby Blue, having my hair touched without anyone asking my permission."

On the other hand, I liked the attention, which was something I hadn't gotten a lot of, in a positive way, for months. There was something soothing, even kind, about the way those women gathered around me, stroking, talking, enjoying the camaraderie. I didn't feel judged.

"I thought Latinx people had blow hair—you know, straight hair—too. Interesting. But get to the story! You are so stubborn like that." Ruby Blue feigns annoyance, but is being playful at the same time.

"Maybe I've taken on some of Fred's ways. While he lived on the reservation, he learned a lot about the American Indians he was working with, and learning from. Storytelling. The stories he brought home were entangled. They swirled into a large, sometimes smokey, circle, but at the end, they always came back to the beginning.

"Kahlil Gibrán, a favorite author of mine, wrote, 'When you reach the end of what you should know, you will be at the beginning of what you should sense....How shall my heart be unsealed unless it be broken? Only great sorrow or great joy can reveal your truth.'"

Again adjusting her position on the couch and tugging on the crocheted blanket. "This blanket isn't especially warm with all the holes. Just sayin'. No, say what? Gilbran who? Stop! No more teacher-mode. Just tell me."

"You know, I've never told anyone this story before. Please be patient with me. The memories feel as though they come in slow motion."

"My bad. You right."

Geeze, I'm just tryin' to hear pieces of Zoe's story! I wanna get to know her better. See the bigger picture. She knows about me but never really talks about herself, beneath the surface, at least...

"Have some more water."

Ruby Blue gives Zoe a long, straight-on stare as she moves her hand in a circular, keep-it-movin' gesture.

"The ramshackle home was in a residential area. Large. Khaki paint peeling. There were eight bedrooms. It might have been a rooming house once. Two girls to a room. Met my first cockroach there. We each had cleaning duties we had to attend to, and we had to make our beds and keep our spaces tidy every day."

This was contentious for some of the girls who had never had to follow these Anglo-Saxton-type rules before, the different cultural expectations. The girls were seen to be at fault if they didn't meet the daily goals because they didn't 'work hard enough' and hard work—by their definition—was seen to be the key to success by the church people who ran the home. Of course, I did not know all of this then; but the rules fit with my upbringing so were easy expectations for me and likely why I was given privileges. The rules and the restrictions created tensions in the house. I stayed completely out of it.

Slightly sarcastic, "How lucky. I get to be trapped in a layin' position all the time."

I wonder what Zoe is thinking about as she tells me this story. Is it painful or is she healing? I can never tell because when I look at her face, it is emotionless. I'm so glad I have Zoe and I don't have to go through the same thing she did, and I get to keep my baby.

"I like having you here, even with me doing some caretaking." The English teacher in Zoe briefly wanders off to a literary passage about caretaking. But she checks herself, not saying the words aloud.

There was an idea from de Saint-Exupery's book, The Little Prince. *I liked teaching that book. It was about building a relationship. Something like, I am just a fox like a hundred thousand other foxes. But if you tame me, we shall need one another. To me, you will be unique. And I shall be unique to you. What does "tame" mean, I now wonder? Forced into my accepted mold? I don't think so, and yet...feel the two of us becoming unique to each other. Truly seeing each other. Maybe embracing differences. I'll think more about this later.*

Shared smiles pass between the women as they dip their heads closer, with slight nods and a little laugh, realizing they are again adding more intimacy, more deepening in their relationship.

Continuing. "The girls in the home were all pregnant and showing except one. She was the palest of Whites, translucent as we have discussed. Her skin was taut across prominent cheek bones. She might have weighed 90 pounds and was probably 13 years old. It seemed she was pregnant because she was in the home, but I could see her hip bones protruding, so maybe three months along. I felt sorry for her. She wasn't my roommate; I don't remember who was.

"Most of the girls were Latinx or mixed race. Because my parents were so disappointed that I was going to a maternity home rather than to college, I asked the house mother if I could attend the local community college, enrolling after the semester was well underway. She and the Board agreed, so off I'd go on the bus each morning. I only had one maternity outfit—the pink and white stripes did not go around me like the design on your top—and I would wash it each evening, then wear it to school again the next day. It was like a self-punishment of sorts, I suppose. But not conscious at that time.

"When people in my classes occasionally asked about my husband, assuming I was married and I did wear a gold band—which I still have—by the way, I'd say he was military and stationed out of the country. That was a reasonable answer because Fort Sam Houston was a nearby military base."

"Why did you pretend you were married?" Ruby Blue innocently asks.

"The stigma. But we can talk more about that later. It wasn't like today. There was tremendous social pressure not to be pregnant out of wedlock, as they used to say.

"If I had to choose one memory to depict the shameful nature of the experience, it would be the day we went to the medical clinic, like a line of ducks waddling in step. All 16 of us were taken for assessment. Wearing our fake wedding rings, we were paraded through the clinic lobby as a group and every eye—I mean every eye—was on us. Obviously, we were pregnant teenagers. We were there to be tested for

STDs. Sexually transmitted diseases. It was truly one of the great embarrassing moments in my life, then."

> *The memory of that experience is visceral and I realize how I have pushed it (and many of these incidents) down, away, for all these years. Now, listening to and being with Ruby Blue I can relate, even if slightly, to some of the stories of prejudice. I had never connected my own life experiences with those of persons of color... is that the correct term? This one humiliating experi- ence was an anomaly for me. For her, adversity can be the daily expectation, if not the everyday experience.*

Ruby Blue nods, showing she knows about embarrassing moments.

"The home was like a prison and no unchaperoned trips were allowed. No boyfriends could visit. I was the only girl allowed to go to college and just one other woman was permit- ted to leave the home unattended. She was my only friend. White like me. Even in a setting like that I had White privi- lege, I now better understand. That privilege distanced me from the other girls too. My advantages accentuated their disadvantages, something I did not fully realize because I had always had advantages. So, nothing new.

"I studied English, history, and German that semester at the community college. I earned an A in English, a C in history and an F in German. Those grades did not help me much, but they did show where my innate talents lay, I suppose.

"My daily pattern in the home was to wash and iron that one maternity outfit, as I've said. Then lie in the sun to study and get tan—so it might look like I'd been away at college playing and partying when I got back home. Ride the bus to and from classes. And then take walks."

> *I'd lie on the cracked concrete driveway—which was so Texas hot that I needed to spread out a towel to keep from getting physically burned—inside the tall, wooden-fenced backyard near the foul garbage bins, while my maternity outfit dried, in minutes, on the clothesline. There were robes in the closet for girls who had no appropriate clothing and I'd wear one of those, hiking it up to expose my skin to the broiling Texas sun. There was peace in that daily ritual, at least during the week. Alone. All I wanted was to be alone. So ashamed. I simply could not connect with the girls in the home. Why? We were all pregnant but somehow my sin felt larger to me. Another kind of judgment, I am now thinking.*

"I bet you were safe walking in that neighborhood, being a White woman, even though you were pregnant and alone," Ruby Blue reflects. "Oh, I'm sorry; I wasn't trying to come at you; I'm just sayin'."

"That's okay, I understand. You're right, you know..."

Continuing. "I made that one friend at the home, as I said. This woman was older than the rest of us. She was married, I learned over time, and had other children. This baby was not her husband's child. She did not want anyone to know. Since then, I have wondered if she was going to give birth to a Black or Brown baby. She had told her family she was going to take a few months away and figure out the rest of her life. They thought she was on a retreat or sabbatical or some such. She had a car, so would take the two of us to safe places to walk, like the zoo for example. We were the only ones allowed to leave like that.

"I did not say more than the minimum number of words to anyone in my classes. I did not talk much with the other girls in the home."

"Oh my gosh, I know! It's like pullin' teeth to get you to talk!" Ruby Blue rolls her eyes, with a smile.

"Yeah, yeah, yeah...anyways, I talked some with the housemother, who was a deeply kind, warm, padded, mothering woman who lived in the home with us all. And then this one friend. Interesting, I never found out her real name. One day, just after she had had her baby and was packing to leave, she showed me an envelope addressed to her. I was too shy, or something, to look at the envelope, so have never known who she was. Someone important, I think. Someone formally educated, for sure."

Pausing and reflecting silently. Remembering.

So, so ashamed. My parents never talked about the home or the decision to give away my son. Their choice actually. I do not remember being part of the decision. I do remember standing in a courtroom where a judge, looking down at me from his dais, asked, "Do you realize what decision you are making?"

"Yes."

Actually, I had no clue. Just being the obedient daughter. Nothing. It was as if nothing external had happened, except, for me, internally, I was forever changed. Terrified of giving birth again. Not feeling I was deserving of having children. My family's mantra was tomorrow will be better—just ignore the past.

"So, you two just walked and talked? Or did anything else happen'?" Ruby Blue tries to get Zoe to go beneath the surface-level chit-chat.

"Yes. We walked and talked, rather she talked, and I asked questions. She had more influence on me than she will ever know. She talked about books. Ideas like existentialism and Marxist philosophy. Writers like Erich Fromm, Viktor Frankl, Simone de Beauvoir, Kahlil Gibrán, and Jean-Paul Sartre. She wrote out a reading list for me at one point, a list I kept for years.

"On one of our walks, I remember she had purchased new shoes—stiff brown and white saddle shoes—and wore them for the extra-long walk that day. When we got home, I looked down and was shocked to see her shoes were filled with blood. She hadn't said a thing. Since then, I have thought that she, like me, was punishing herself.

"One of my biggest regrets now is that I listened to her talks for weeks and, at the end of our time, I said to her, 'I think you are all wet.' What a stupid, childish thing to say. I was responding from my very conservative upbringing; was saying what my parents would have said, them honoring their world based on White history and male leaders. Their beliefs enter into what I'm telling you too because they did not believe in discussing personal life or expressing intimacy. Above all, avoid conflict!

"Since then, I have studied the people and philosophies she talked about and found brilliance in what I learned from her. Then, I knew not I knew not.

"She did not talk to me much after my inconsiderate, rude comment."

Stretching but not changing position much, not wanting to interrupt Zoe's monologue, Ruby Blue encouraged her to continue. "So, you had the baby and..."

"Wait a sec, Ruby Blue, there is more. After my only friend had her baby, and after I had rejected her ideas, she went for walks alone. Runs, actually. In those same bloody shoes, and now I expect she was also bleeding post-birth. Her baby was given up for adoption. Then she was just gone. But her ideas remained and pushed me toward my college teaching career. I never got to thank her."

If I had looked at her name on that envelope, would I have someday contacted her again? If asked, how would I explain how I'd known her? She did trust, or try to trust, me enough to reveal who she was. I was such a brat—a scared, humiliated, beaten-down brat.

"So, then you had your baby and..."

"So many questions from you, Ruby Blue! Aannddd, I was sitting at the long table in the kitchen with the other girls and the house mother. Lunch time. The labor pains had started but I thought they were just cramps, like a band tightening around my belly. Finally, I realized something more might be happening and I got up and walked over to the nurturing house mother and whispered to her, 'I think I might be in labor.' I had no real way of knowing, but figured it was labor when I saw her nod.

"She took me to my room, where we got my bag and off we went to the hospital. The home had no education on childbirth and I did not know anything about birthing—which we will make sure doesn't happen for you. But the baby was born. I gave him up for adoption. I went home and spent the summer like other college kids. And in the fall, I went off to a regular four-year college. But, as I said, I was emotionally older than the other students. I had been in a different place. I was more serious, I guess."

Zoe pauses in telling her story, taking a breath.

> *Is it really worthwhile to bring these memories up again? To what end? Why does Ruby Blue want to know these things? Perhaps it is the fear of birthing that is driving her questions. The nose ring—to cut the pain— is an indication of her fear, now that I think about it.*

> *In truth, that summer after my son was born, I went rogue. I had dates every night, often more than one per evening, partying and much more. Promiscuous. I didn't care about anything. I felt less than, something Ruby Blue could relate to, but I won't tell her this. Yes, residue from my staid up-bringing. How incredibly long these mores of childhood stay with us. I mean, my parents have been dead for decades, I have no siblings, and even Fred is dead. Now, no one knows—or cares— about this story, this experience. Although, out there somewhere, is that child I gave birth to and gave away. Somewhere. Probably.*

"But what about the birth?" Ruby Blue's brow furrows, concerned. "I'm afraid of the birthing. I've heard stories. Do you think I can do this?"

> *Will my knife nose ring really help to cut the pain or is that some sort of superstition? Will Marcus be with me? I guess not, with Covid. And this jail situation. At least*

I know Zoe will be there for me. No, she'll be there for us.

"Yes, birthing hurts. I was so naïve I did not know it would be painful. But women give birth all the time and survive, so I know you, as a strong Black woman, can do anything.

"The house mother stayed with me as long as she could and we talked. She was kind. And then the boy was born. And that was that. The nurses wrapped a long band around my chest, pressing my breasts in, after I was given an injection to stop my milk from coming. This won't happen for you, though."

"Did you see him? The baby, I mean."

I can't even imagine giving my daughter away. I do not understand how she could have done something like this.

Speaking more rapidly now, as the memories flood in, Zoe adds, "A nurse made a mistake and brought him to me while I was in the hospital—back then, women stayed in the hospital for days after giving birth. I held him for about five minutes but then another nurse, who knew better, came and whisked him away from me. Abruptly. Scowling."

"Did you ever try to find him?"

"I did. I was told that he had died; that I had given birth to both life and death."

"Did you believe them?"

"No, but what recourse did I have?" Zoe sighs. "This was all before there was an Internet and many states had regulations about not disclosing information to birth mothers. It was, I suppose, a way to protect the babies and the adoptive families. It was also another way to punish the birth mothers, I think."

We are getting too close to some painful truths here.
Time to move on.

"Hmm. Okay. Thanks for the very detailed, but special story. I think I would have made friends with the other women there because we would all have been in the same place," Ruby Blue reflects.

"You are right about that. I felt I was different, and in many ways, I was. Not better. Just different. But I expect my actions and attitudes did come off as me feeling I was superior. Shyness mixed with shame can lead to that feeling of distancing."

"In my community, when babies are born to unmarried women, they are not adopted away like your baby was," Ruby Blue considers. "I wonder why? Maybe those children were not thought to be desirable for adoption or maybe the families just cherished them so much that giving them away was not an option. Could it have been a post-slavery thing from when children were just taken away and sold? Alright, anyways, thanks for telling me more. I wonder if your baby did die or if they were just trying to destroy your hope?"

Ignoring Ruby Blue's question, Zoe changes the subject. "Okay, time for bed! Let me help you carry the preg pillow."

WONDER, WOMAN

Telling her story of the home for unwed mothers was exhausting. Zoe returns to her striped chair and starts to lower herself with grace—as she had been taught to do as a girl, one leg back, one forward—then pauses and lets her body drop down into the comfort. The silence and familiarity are reassuring. She looks around at the old-fashioned living room with its worn and eclectic, but clean, furniture. There are knick-knacks—bits and pieces that hold memories from travels and adventures—things that would mean nothing to others and likely are seen merely as objects to be dusted. She loves them all. Her treasures.

On the far wall, where the afternoon sun warms it, is the stylized Native American painting given to Fred many years before, on the reservation when he was honored at a pow-wow. They both cherished it; now she alone did.

The pale auburn background shows echoes of rock art designs in crimson and turquoise. Foreground? Dark shadow shapes. Two adults, standing. A bear following a star. His star? Two blackbirds facing each other and perhaps conversing. And a cornstalk with small plants at the base that could be the early stages of beans and squash. The Three Sisters. A painting depicting the fundamental elements of living, of life. Honored history. Desire. Procreation. Unity. Interconnectedness.

Sitting alone, Zoe ponders.

There was that time on the reservation when a sandy cat pressed against my chest, wanting attention, and I realized breasts can be warm pillows; not only for feeding but simply for offering comfort. Then it occurred to me that I had no memory of my mother ever holding me next to her breasts. She must have when I was a tiny baby. But nothing in conscious memory.

I had taken those ten students to live with families on Fred's one-million-acre reservation for a week. The students were spread out everywhere. It was stressful, even with Fred as guide.

One late afternoon, the mother of the woman whose house I was staying at was sitting on the couch watching me. She sensed the degree of my stress and patted the couch next to her. I sat down, properly distanced. She patted the couch again, closer to her. I scooted over and she put her arm around my shoulders and pulled me in close. At first, I resisted. But then I leaned in and she pulled my head, gently, to her pillowy shoulder; her bulk spilling over onto me. I completely gave in to her nurturing and we sat in that quiet way for a long time. It was the most mothering moment of my life. And that from a stranger.

I want Ruby Blue to have a warmly painted memory from this time in her life, like Gal Gadot said of giving birth. She felt such strength, like she was a goddess. She looked at the baby and said, 'Oh, my God, I made this." She truly was Wonder Woman in those moments. That is what I want for Ruby Blue.

Beyond this place, however, there can be dragons.

Being a pregnant teen can feel like losing everything one had hoped or imagined for the future. How do you reimagine that hope? How do you find a place to stop so you can start again? A place of silence. A person to trust. A place of privacy to step away from the demands of society. And maybe this isn't what Ruby Blue is feeling. Maybe this was just what I experienced in my too young pregnancy. Remembering for me is never an act of quiet reflection. It is a painful retelling.

I will never tell Ruby Blue the rest of my story. I wrote it once. Right now, I am thinking about a scene in Toni Morrison's book, Beloved. *Paul D, a slave, was walking past a rooster named Mister. Paul D had a bit in his mouth, punishment from the slave master. There was Mister, standing in a coop, on a tub in the sun. Paul D realized that that rooster was freer than he was. Paul D was dehumanized, had to be considered less than fully human for democracy and Christianity to be moral. Mister got to be, and stay, who he was. Even if he was cooked, you would still be cooking a rooster named Mister. Paul D could never again be who and what he had been born to be. Slavery and incarceration had changed him forever.*

The rest of my story changed me forever, giving me acute awareness; I cannot even imagine what the collective slave memories have done to generations of people. The cruelties.

I once walked into a visual art display by chance. A chessboard base filled the room. Life-sized manikins were positioned on it like chess pieces. Some had on nurse outfits. One was dressed like a doctor, with a stethoscope draped casually around his neck. Others were helpers, maybe like social workers. There was one, solitary, single, girl figure—not even a woman yet. I walked among the figures, back and forth. Then around the edges of the whole display. The artist had shared my experiences. I knew.

On a table, there was an artist's comment book. No one else was in the room. I sat on a worn stair, examining dirt that had been missed by a custodian's broom, caught around the edges, and wrote six pages in that book in a stiff, tight handwriting. Then I left the book and walked away. I did not sign my name.

What I wrote was the rest of my story.

Before I lay talking with the kind house mother, I was taken to a hospital room with a high ceiling, and put on a table. An efficient aide shaved my pubic hair after lathering me with cold, white shaving cream, which I understand people do now for whatever reasons—erotic, I guess. But I was humiliated. The person with the shaver was rough with me and left several raw, scraped areas. Then someone inserted an enema tube. I'd never had one before, didn't even know what it was, so did not know what to expect. Apparently, it was believed that the baby could be infected during birth from fecal bacteria.

There was a row of bathroom doors along one wall, white enamel paint and each with an old-fashioned prism-glass doorknob, like my Grammy had in her house. Seeking release, my brain flashed to remembering Grammy, stodgy, gray hair secured in a disorderly tangle, clumping around in her dull slippers, patting the pockets of her flowered housedress, trying to remember where she left the matches needed to light the old stove. A warming comfort. A wish she was here now.

Harshly, the nurse commanded me to go into one of the bathroom stalls and wait for the enema to work. I did. The pain rapidly became unbearable. Blood was flowing hard. I got up, wearing my skimpy hospital gown, open in the back, and limped to the hallway to call for help.

I was so scared.

I could see the nurses down the hall, standing together and laughing. It seemed like they were a block away. I tried to call out to them, but they did not look toward me, or seem to hear me. Blood and enema and more were gushing down my legs. The room, in my memory, had a pock-marked concrete floor and shiny brick walls. White. It was large. The only furniture I remember was that stainless steel table I had been put on for the enema.

Cold.

The cold was knifing in.

Everything was so cold.

I was in unimaginable pain. I walked to the corner of the room and slid down. The hospital gown rode up. Bared skin. Sitting. More cold. The floor was cold. I slid sideways and curled into a fetal position, a grief curl. I lay there, crying and bleeding. Moaning aloud, low, like an animal.

I can never excuse the cruelty, even violence, of the hospital staff on a 17-year-old child. Me. It was not their job to punish me for my perceived sins. Women scorning their own. Hadn't they ever faced something like this before? For me, in my mind, this will never be alright. It couldn't be.

These memories are bringing tears. Why am I having to remember all of this again?

A nurse came in after a while. I have no idea how long I lay curled in that corner. She got me up on that table again, "Get on the table." So cold. I was so cold. Wet. So wet. She wheeled me to another part of the delivery area. How long had this been going on? I was thirsty. Shaking.

They gave me a blanket that helped as I talked with the kind house mother for just a few minutes. Then she left. I never saw her again.

The pain got intense again. I was wheeled into the delivery room on an examining table with one wheel that shook, stuttered; I suppose that was what it was. No one talked to me. I wonder if the medical folks felt a moral injury for what they did to, and didn't do for, me? But I suppose they felt it was fitting since I had committed an ethical transgression and was probably a social deviant in their eyes. I'll never know.

I felt so utterly alone and, at the same time, the center of attention. I did not know anyone. I'd never met the doctor. I was in unbelievable pain, as if anything I'd ever experienced before had been a two and this was a fifty-seven. It hurt like nothing else I knew, in my chest, behind my eyes, everywhere. And then they put my legs up in stirrups. And then strapped my legs tightly to the metal. Then they strapped down my arms. Tethered. Shackled. Unable to move and in agony. I struggled and struggled.

I remember the moment I pulled one hand free. I just wanted to have that tiny amount of control. The only words that come in my memory are, "Get that hand. Strap her down again. Tighter." The doctor's gruff harsh words.

I read later that women's hands and feet were re-strained because the narcotics given for pain caused agitation. Writhing that was so violent there was danger of falling off the delivery table. Well, with me, that wasn't an issue because I do not remember having drugs, even for the episiotomy—when they cut my vagina opening to give the baby more room to be born. If any drugs were supposed to blunt my memory of the events, either they did not work or those particular drugs were not administered to me.

The pain was so intense I literally went blind. Pain as fire. Pain as drowning. My eyes were open but every-thing was black.

Then the pain stopped and I thought it was over. Except the pains started again. Afterbirth. No one told me anything. I was panicked. I truly thought I was dying, maybe wishing for that relief.

I was shaking and shivering with a mix of fear, pain, and the feel of scowls surrounding me. I was wet all over, drenched. Even my pores were crying.

* * *

I had already signed papers for the adoption, but one nurse did not see the notation (maybe), so brought the baby to me. I held him for a few minutes before another nurse came in and briskly whisked him away. Frown-ing, fuming. Imagine the feeling of holding your child outside of your body for the first time.

They gave me an injection to stop my breasts from producing milk and wrapped a tight Ace bandage around me. No one asked me if I wanted that, and I did not know what they were doing. Mostly I was passive and so sad. Several times, though, I walked down the hall to the area where the babies were displayed. I looked at him through the window. My son.

Someone mumbled at me, "This child will go to a good home, better than you could ever provide."

Thinking back on all of this, I believe the nurses, and even the doctor, were punishing me. They did not know that I had already punished myself enough. There was no tenderness or caring at any point during the birthing, or after. Now I sometimes watch movies about birthing centers and doulas and warm baths and soft music and am glad for today's moms. This is what I hope Ruby Blue experiences. Can that happen during Covid?

That pregnancy and birth impacted me forever. It was the loss of childhood. I could not return to school and be like my peers because I was older in life lived than they were. I isolated from them. I don't know for sure all of what it has meant, other than that Fred and I never had children. And I surely am not going to tell Ruby Blue any of this story, this life-changing experience. I was just her age. I was just her young age.

Once in a while something triggers a snippet of memory and I retell the story to myself, not because I have to remember, but because I'll never be able to forget. Birthing is the woman's story. I would like to believe that I did the right thing in giving my son two parents who loved him and gave him an awesome life. Later, I learned that it was standard practice to place babies to be adopted in a home where they were boarded for several months before being given to the adoptive family, to ensure the child was healthy, I suppose. A good adoptable baby.

A thing I did not understand until recently was that adoption was a big business during the 60s. People wanted babies. White babies. Social curses on unmarried women provided the raw material—children—to be sold. Between 1944 and 1975, close to three million adoptions occurred. Like the pipeline to prison that caught Marcus, the adoption market was its own legal profitable pipeline.

Okay, let's not open that terrifying box further. Put all of this back in the tin strongbox—shaped like my grandfather's Sir Walter Raleigh Tobacco tin that I have long imagined rests in my chest as a dustbin. Snap the corroded lid closed. Lock it away. Maybe forever this time. Done. Well, almost done.

I'm wondering now, after listening to Ruby Blue, if my trauma was just a one-time experience—the one time my privilege did not protect me. There are clearly others who have experienced repeated traumas. I wonder how they deal with it? Is the strongbox in their chests larger than mine, thicker? Are there ways to make this a positive life learning experience? Don't know. That sounds so Pollyanna-ish. But maybe. Or maybe it is too late. Don't know.

"Only if we face these open wounds in ourselves can we understand them in other people," *James Baldwin wrote. Maybe true.*

ANOTHER LETTER

Another letter for you, and I put more money on Marcus' books so he can call you, Ruby Blue."

Dear Ruby Blue: I'm here, 'cause I know you been lookin' for me. Because of Covid lockdown and overcrowding, I was moved from the jail to the prison. I am in one of the new cells. The sink is directly under a very bright LED light, like a stage light. There is a listening device in the cell. The desk is real small. The toilet is right next to the bottom bunk which is a potential issue, privacy, and simply nasty, if one of us gets sick.

Jail or prison, most days still the same as the day before. Time doesn't move in either place. It doesn't even stand still. But now we are two guys to a cell rather than them bunk beds. I hear they are even doubling guys up in the punishment segregation cells. Imagine that! A shower once a week. Push button for three minutes, then off. Repeat. All meals in the cell. No recreation. It gets real real boring. I guess that's what they call doing time. I'm trying to be the best version of myself though it's difficult with the kind of books they got here, like A Short Introduction to the History of Chemistry. Lots of time in the cell because of staff shortages. More than is recommended, I guess. Not my choice. But I gotta buck up.

Sometimes there is action.

My cellie is this self-proclaimed genius who collects numbers and quotes, like, 'One in three ninjas end up in prison.' That's me. I'm special – one out of three. Not a good joke. He says homeboys are six times more likely than honkies to get incarcerated with 20% longer sentences. Truly, I don't like bein' somebody's statistic or prediction, but haven't been sentenced yet, so don't know. Dude had a whole melt down and in the midst of the rant about his girlfriend, he says, "Yeah, I know I shot her in the head, but it was an accident plus it was her fault, I was trying to shoot someone else and she got in the way, so if she knows it was an accident why the fuck is she still trippin'."

When I get out, he says, me and you are gonna struggle to get a crib or SNAP or that student loan for me. It's rigged, but that ain't stoppin' us. We will overcome!

He says it's the emotions I need to watch. Prison isn't so much about body – they don't take us out back and whip us anymore like in slave times -- but the soul, they attack. I'm supposed to be deprived of freedom, not deprived of humanity. What does that mean? Don't really wanna know.

I see cold grayness in this place. Doors slammin'. A strange, sort of out of control feeling when they first took my shoelaces and belt and I had to shuffle around holding up my jeans. Maybe that's the soul taking a beatdown. I felt like a kid.

So, the action? They had a nine-person brawl yesterday, during the only rec this week. This guard, who twitches every time he thinks he hears somethin', was on duty. About a month ago, maybe longer, I heard he was on the scene and there was a string of fights almost every weekend. Then he was gone a long time. Things calmed down. A few days ago, he pops up again telling prisoners, 'Take this down!', 'Move that!', 'Give me this!', 'Give me that!', blah blah blah. This guard creates discomfort and tension and more fights. He comes around early when most guys are sleepin' to enforce some stupid non-security rule. Within a few days of him being back there has been two fights, one being the nine-person brawl. People ran just to join in the fight. Somethin' to do.

And then there is this other guy, a prisoner – they call us inmates, but we are really prisoners because we don't want to be here and are imprisoned – who has nothing. No TV, no radio, nothing. By choice. Says he is a voodoo practitioner. By having nothing, he has control. No guard can work toward taking anything away from him because there is nothing to take, even though a prisoner has nothing that is truly his own anyway. He says that, years ago, if you had too much of anything, like T-shirts or socks, they let you choose the option to send home whatever you couldn't have. But here they keep it all to replenish their own shelves. They passed out leaflets saying that they will come around this weekend to do cell searches, to give us a chance to dump our contraband—no questions asked. But, starting Monday, they gonna grab the prison by its ankles and shake out whatever's left. Not an issue for me 'cause I'm like dude, and don't have more than soap and toothpaste and a brush. Be interesting anyway.

And then another guy who cries every night at 9pm. Every night. He and his cuz were drinkers. Heavy. They would finish off their day supply and then get more for the evening. They would fight and carry on, but they loved each other. Best friends. One night, 9pm, a drunken fight and dude stabbed his cuz, who died. Now, every night he cries because he lost his best friend.

And, I see it. Family breakdown. Many men here had fathers in prison, a mom on drugs, and they learned about relationships and women and men from movies and music videos and social media. Guys talk about their Granny being heroin addicts or crack heads, like they criminals rather than they got a health problem. But when I was a kid, Grannies and Big Mommas were everything. It was unthinkable that anybody's Granny could be an addict.

Anyway, enough on me, how ya doin? Zoe? She good for you? Our seed, what are we gonna name her? I love you, Baby. We sure will be good. Be strong.

Love you, my queen, my Ruby Blue
Your Black King ♥

As Ruby Blue was reading, she was stroking her distended belly. Caressing the baby. Soothing her. Now, she stands up and reaches for Marcus' hoodie that she brought with her from that apartment where she was abandoned, when all she wanted was to go home, but there was no other place to go to. She buries her nose and smells deeply of her love. His scent is still there. Recognizable.

Damn I miss my man. Damn.

ECONOMIC POVERTY

Thanks. I might be getting use' to yo healthy food, or maybe it is just havin' you doing all the cookin.' I like that fish 'n the strawberries. You can eat all the squash for us both. Thanks anyway; you are like warm bread to me."

Although, I must say I am a way better cook than you with yo crooked-ass food and raw vegetables!

"I wonder how me and Marcus are going to do with the baby. We will taste the joys for sure, but have you ever been poor, Zoe?"

Smiling at the ease of the question and the familiarity, "I like being like warm bread for us both! No, Ruby Blue, I have never been in that situation for real, economic poverty. Seems to me like there are different kinds of poverty. Poverty of spirit or soul. Poverty of kindness. Poverty of love. I always had family I knew I could turn to, even if they showed no emotion, if I needed something basic like a place to live or food or even a car. But I think I know that, in final estimation, we are all humans. More connects us than separates us. Fred knew this."

"You are lucky, Zoe. The people I was staying with were poor. I was poorer 'cause I had nothing after Marcus got locked up. But I knew poverty even before. It is like passed down from one generation to the next and something like

Marcus being a felon now will set us up, maybe. You inherit this sugar bowl and I inherit poverty. Wanna trade?"

Kindly, hesitantly, Zoe asks, "Did you get to finish high school?"

Pausing and wondering if there is judgment in the way the question is worded, but finding none, Ruby Blue answers, "I finished high school early, taking pre-college AP classes. I'd be in college now, if the loan promises had been real. But Covid. Damn Covid. And I really want to travel and look all around, like you got to do, before. All over the United States and everywhere. Well, maybe not North Dakota and Kansas, but I don't know for sure."

Smiling, nodding, Zoe responds, "Travel is something I do love, like you. And I'm smiling because Fred spent a lot of time in North Dakota and we treasured that rugged place. And there is Underground Railroad history and the Flint Hills with grasses that can grow ten feet tall in Kansas. Haunting! Who knew?"

"Where all have you been? And do you miss Fred?" Ruby Blue extends the conversation to avoid, for the moment, having to lie down again.

"Yes, I miss Fred, like you are missing Marcus, I think. At least Marcus will be coming back to you. Fred and I didn't get to travel together too much because our jobs and work were so far apart. We intended to go to Alaska after we retired, but that didn't happen. It is the one state I've never been to, but I've touched a toe in the other 49, at least. And most continents too. Travel taught me the U.S. is not the center of the globe like it was suggested in school. Important humbling lesson."

"Did you know there is dust in poor people's houses that hangs in the air? I've seen it," Ruby Blue points out as she looks around. "No dust here."

"I kind of know about that dust from travels in the third world, Zoe recalls. Once I was looking for a mailbox in a third-world city. I was illiterate, meaning I couldn't read the signs that were not written in English. I found a symbol that looked to me like it meant post office and the door was open, so I walked into the large room. There were people sitting on chairs around the gritty edges, separated but all facing toward the center. Footprint tracks in the dust followed the swale suggesting I move toward a back room. The seated people looked at me strangely and gestured that I should follow the dust trail. I did and a man who spoke English came toward me. I explained that I was looking to buy postcard stamps for the U.S. and the mail slot and he said, "You are standing in my living room. Leave now. The post office is down the street."

Ruby Blue giggles, "Funny! You were the fool." The women share a good, healing laugh. Another bridge.

Wanting to continue their moments together, the coffee, the upright position, and pleased to have found topics Zoe will talk more about and feeling progressively secure in asking, Ruby Blue questions, "How about a tough experience?"

Pausing, then thinking which transformative experience to talk about, realizing how lucky she is to be able to select among many, Zoe recalls, "My students and I were walking down a street in Amsterdam, Red Light District, where a person could find anything they'd want.

"At the end of the street, we saw a series of two-story, full-size windows. On the second floor, women on rope swings were rocking back and forth through open windows above the street. Back and forth. On the first floor, women were sitting, exposed, behind each window selling their bodies to anyone who was buying. There was a single bed and a curtain behind each woman. It was completely shocking to me, and I was so upset walking past these desperate prostitutes. At the last door, a very young woman stood, high-heel rocked to one side, one foot half behind her, tentative and scared-looking. She was wearing a too-tight yellow dress. Stained. She was crying. I wanted to take her away, but how? I just walked on by, averting my eyes."

The students with me had been joking about the openness on the street until they, too, saw this young woman, about their ages. They got somber really fast. It was a teaching moment I did not know how to deal with.

"Do you think I should have tried to do something? What? I have wondered."

Firmly, Ruby Blue offers, "I used to believe that everyone who hurt me still loved me but now I understand that some were preying on me. Exploiting me. In the hood, you are either predator or prey, but I'm stronger now because of it. I don't know how you could have helped her though. Up to her to help herself."

* * *

It was another pandemic day. There was nothing on their agenda other than more eating; nothing pressing, nothing needing to be done. Covid had changed the pace of life. Some people fought this. Some people relaxed into the new pace, as Zoe and Ruby Blue did, whether a conscious choice or not. Just continuing their chatting.

"What would you do, if someone gave you a $100 bill when you needed money, Ruby Blue?"

"Well, you can't understand my kind of poverty. Embarrassin' poverty where you have to fight from the sidelines, from the edges, 'cause you never mainstream. Where would I go with that kind of money? If I tried to spend it, White folks would want to know my whole life story, like they were sure I stole it. They would want to see my driver's license or photo ID but even then, they'd assume I stole it. They would mark the bill with one of those invisible pens. Maybe they would change it, but probably just send me away. Or worse, call the cops. That is poverty. That is also race. Discrimination. You don't know this. How could you? You're White. A White woman at that. You got it so much better than the rest of us Black women have it."

Moving back to the living room where Ruby Blue could lie down on the comfortable couch, and leaving the lunch dishes on the table—healthy eating was what the women were mostly doing these days in the time of thisday, thatday, otherday, someday, yesterday, today, and nextday, as the joke goes. Zoe continues.

"The one thing I know is age discrimination. Inside my little world, I do what makes me happy. I work on being sensitive, but not soft, or vulnerable. I am visible to me. But then, out in the world, my wrinkles seem to make me disappear one groove at a time. I become invisible. A woman of my age that nobody much looks at, other than that time we were in the protest, demanding help.

"One time, a few years ago, I decided to test whether people actually saw me. I went to a little county fair with lots of animals and a carnival fairway. I walked around alone. I stood really close to a group of men who were talking with each other about cows. Too close. They should have been uncomfortable, but they never looked my way.

"Then I walked down the center of the arcade area where young people were flocking. I could walk right toward the groups, and they would part like the proverbial Red Sea. No one acknowledged me.

"Finally, I stood next to children lined up waiting to get on a kiddy ride. Again, no one was looking until suddenly one child, maybe six years old, looked me full in the face and smiled this great grin. She was the only person who truly saw me all day. I smiled back. An innocent child saw beyond my wrinkles."

Nodding and caressing the side of her belly, Ruby Blue adds, "Okay, so invisible. I sort of get that, although my problem is that I'm too visible. The people I was staying with got several minimum-wage jobs, called front-line during this Covid time, and then moved from part-time to full-time. When that happened, they lost their SNAP benefits, and the rent went from $475 to $950. They could not afford rent, food, and healthcare, so tried to self-heal with herbs and Ibuprofen. If I had been with them and had this preeclampsia, my baby and I could have died. Should I be more afraid of hospitals and doctors who see, but ignore, me, or should I be more afraid of poverty that sidelines me? Or all of this?"

"I don't know the answers, Ruby Blue. Wish we could solve these things together. But my eyes are getting heavy now. How about we let this rest for the time being, and take our naps? Good for us both, from what I read about you being pregnant and know about being old!"

I wonder what I'd be doing right now if Fred were alive? A nap together, resting like spoons? Would my life be much different, day to day, than it is now? I wonder. Fred would like her. I am progressively more and more sure.

"Yes, we will sleep. Maybe Marcus will call again tonight. Don't let the bedbug's bite!"

SEARCHING FOR ZOE'S SON

Stretching her arms toward the Cuppa Joe wallpaper border next to the ceiling and again enjoying a little time out of bed or off of the couch, Ruby Blue offers, "The days are blurring. You know, we got all this time, just sittin' around. Why don't we see if we can find your son who was adopted?"

Zoe silently questions herself,

> *Do I want to do this? What good could come from finding him at this point? I named him David. I wonder what his adoptive parents named him? Did he live?*

"Well, I did work on that a little bit once. The records I found are in a drawer in the back room—the ones that said he had died," Zoe nods toward the doorway behind her.

Ruby Blue twists and looks down the hallway toward her room. "I thought you did not have access to information because of agency policies. How on earth did you manage to do that!?"

"I remembered the name of the agency that handled the adoption, but the records were closed in Texas. Mine was church-sponsored, not a state-run baby broker, but a broker nonetheless. I even tried finding his birth certificate, but did not have enough information. I know the adoption agencies sealed them, changing the name given to the child by the birth mother. They even routinely changed the date and city of birth and nothing indicated that the certificates were not the originals. That made it very difficult for the birth mother or first mother or natural mother or whatever name was assigned to me, to trace, and I suppose that is the point. And then I read that some children, especially males, do not want to discover more about their identity, maybe feeling they are betraying their adoptive parents. Makes sense, I suppose. There is no relationship with me. His first question might well be, 'Why did you give me away?'" Zoe looks down. "What do I answer to that? Do I say, 'I was young'? 'Cultural pressures?' Sound like excuses to me."

Shrugging her right shoulder as she dutifully lies down on the couch, Ruby Blue questions, "Well, there could be a relationship. How do you know he doesn't want to meet you? How do you know if you don't try? What if you knew he wanted to meet you? Would you want to meet him then?"

Following Ruby Blue to the living room and automatically bending to pick up a piece of lint she spotted on the rug, Zoe adds, "A thing to understand, as I have said, is that that was a different time. Enduring Victorian beliefs from the earlier generation, I suppose. Societal control over sex. But babies were desirable and unwed mothers were not. So, discrete adoptions were seen as win/win situations. The person who was left out was the birth mother, although I suppose it was felt she could discretely go on with her life without stigma. Lots of young women left home to go live with Aunt Whoever, hiding their pregnancy. And they came home months later with no baby in tow. This whole adoption plan helped the child avoid yet another stigma, that of being illegitimate. Yes, things have changed so dramatically. But the hurt lingers for those of us caught up in that spiteful time."

Pausing and remembering how she and Marcus had joked about being in a contraceptive desert, well, before she got pregnant, that was. "Couldn't you and your guy just have used birth control? Or wrapped it up?"

Zoe shakes her head, "Yeah, well, and that was not legal either, even for some married couples. The whole topic was taboo. Maybe all of this is part of what led to the baby boom following World War II."

Mildly interested, then repositioning her pillow, trying to get comfortable, "What do you mean, baby boom?"

"Have you heard the dismissive phrase, '*Okay, Boomer*'? Younger generations say it to reject or mock unsolicited attitudes professed by my large post-World War II generation. I suppose each generation feels smothered by the previous one, as I did by the sexual Victorian mores I rebelled against. Boomers are coming into our older age now, collectively. Sorry. You may have to work to support us through Social Security payments!" Zoe shrugs her right shoulder in a what-are-you-going-to-do-about-it gesture.

"Yikes. I cannot even support myself," Ruby Blue complains. "Did your mom tell you about pregnancy and this stigma, as you call it?"

Zoe walks over and opens the front door, leaving the aluminum storm door with its pie-crust-edged glass latched and trying to remember where Fred would have put the screen insert. Probably in the garage. She loves these early spring days when the fecund smells rise from the warming earth.

Fred would have been off, preparing for planting on the reservation now. Spring had always been an alone

*time: conclude the semester teaching, dig in the gar-
dens, and deeply breathe the restless awakening smells.
Were pansies and violas and snapdragons and gerani-
ums and those semi-annual dusty millers that she loved
going to be available this year? Had hardy spring
annuals been grown during the Covid winter? Would
their faces turn toward the sun again?*

Refocusing on Ruby Blue's question, Zoe replies. "Those things
were just understood. White husbands were breadwinners—
made the money—and were heads of the household. Women
were homemakers and were subordinate to the male. Ideal
families consisted of two parents and two or three children
who were taught to be independent and all had separate
bedrooms. Sex was never discussed. My mother did not tell me
about menstruation, or what that meant. There was no
Internet. What I knew about puberty I learned from girl-
friends during giggling slumber parties. When I did begin to
bleed, my mother took me into the bathroom, unwrapped a
tampon, and dropped it in the toilet to show me how it could
contain fluid. End of lesson. My girlfriend told me where to
put the thing."

"What did it mean for you to go through puberty?" Ruby
Blue asks while looking intently at Zoe, perhaps for the first
time, seeing parallels in their life stories despite their age
difference.

*I think I can see the girl in this old woman as the light
from the doorway softens and blurs her wrinkles.*

"I was pretty cute—well, getting to be cute." Zoe dips her
head to one side and coyly smiles, reenacting the tempting

gesture she probably used decades before when tantalizing some unsuspecting teen, not even realizing then that she was flirting. "I did not know that things were changing except that I knew my friends were getting bras for their developing breasts. I had none—bras or breasts—but finally asked my mother to buy me a brassiere. She did. The little pointy cups were all wrinkled with nothing to fill them. Funny! I just wanted to be like the other girls and wore a tight elastic girdle like they did. Looking back that is pretty silly because I was rail thin. There was nothing for a girdle to hold in or up. But the girdles had painful little garter buttons that slipped into hoops to hold up the socially mandated nylon stockings."

"Why painful?" Ruby Blue tries to imagine why the buttons hurt while thinking that the maternity pants Eleanor had given her, with their ever-tighter elastic waistbands, were progressively uncomfortable as well.

"Imagine sitting on hard school chairs with buttons cutting into the backs of your legs for hours at a time. Sometimes, fashion can be deeply mindless. What did puberty mean for you?"

Smiling. Thinking of this recent past, Ruby Blue adds, "I was cute too with my little du-rag tied in the front, but not too tight, and my nose stud, left side, that was supposed to ease menstrual cramps. Lots of nerves close to nostrils to be stimulated, in a good way, they say. And my wood and bone African beads—remembering my ancestors—that came from Granny's place after she passed. At least my fashion doesn't hurt...well, didn't hurt before this pregnancy."

Unconsciously disregarding Ruby Blue's complaint about uncomfortable maternity clothes, "Yes, Ruby Blue. Your fashion is smarter than mine! Boys began whistling at me which, I guess, is why I was dressed that way, even though I did not know it. There was no sex education in school. There wasn't a lot of political correctness then either. Lots of misogyny, but of course I did not know what that was. Just normal behavior."

"Misogyny? Like, not valuing women?"

"Yes, and more. Believing that women are inferior to men. Even hating women, which is clearly prejudice. Hating someone for the way they were born, whether skin color or gender or physical difference. Prejudice."

Feeling heartened by the responses she is getting and growing more curious, Ruby Blue asks, "What did you and your guy do? I mean, how did you get pregnant."

Zoe pauses, looking out the storm door, uncomfortable and unsure of what to share with this very young woman.

She is enjoying this conversation more than I am. It is feeling like one of those slumber parties where I learned about sex, wearing my wrinkled pointy bra and painting our fingernails blue. I hope she doesn't ask if I would have gotten an abortion, if that had been a legal possibility. I know I might have, but don't want to tell her that.

Speaking more slowly, Zoe explains, "Well, kind of the usual way. No condoms. Parked cars. Dark nights. Teenage lust. What some called willful intercourse, and, yes, I did want it. I did not really know how babies were conceived, so was not consciously connecting sex with pregnancy. None of it seemed bad because we believed we were in love and I was seeking security. To be hugged. True, if you can believe all of that, and I guess you can. Same story as yours, pretty close, although I expect you are less naïve than I was. And suddenly...well, not even so suddenly because I did not have any idea what was happening, I was nearly five months pregnant before I told my parents and only then beginning to show."

"Were they mad?"

"My parents were sad and, as I've said, did everything they could to hide my shameful pregnancy. Once the baby was born, we never talked about it again. That was how I got moved to Texas to live with Aunt Whomever. Of course, I did not have an aunt in Texas, but that was where the home for unwed mothers was. I had my first gynecologist experience, which was completely humiliating. Like yours was too."

"Hell ya," Ruby Blue recalls the, so recent, feel of the cold, hard stirrups on her heels in Dr. Foster's office.

There is silence as each woman reflects on her own experience. After a few minutes, Zoe adds,

"You know, your situation is different because you have choices about what will happen for your baby. No one ever asked me what I wanted to do. Ruby Blue...Ruby Blue. Are you asleep?"

"Kinda. Resting my eyes."

Zoe walks to the computer while Ruby Blue rests on the couch. She bypasses that adoption information that she knows is in the drawer, taking a new approach. It has been a long time since she tried to find out what happened to her baby and maybe contact him. This time, she just looks up key words: finding adopted child.

* * *

Later. "While you were sleeping, I checked out some information on searching for a child who was adopted. The people who facilitated my adoption are gone. Out of business.

I read up on Texas adoption records and found that they are still sealed by law. Not too surprising. But the adoptee can get a redacted copy of some information."

"Well, you can't go deep on that."

Zoe continues, "The other approach that was suggested was to sign up with a national adoption registry. The one I found is for adoptees, birth mothers and fathers, and siblings, and other family members. It seems pretty comprehensive. So, I will fill out the form, send them $10, and hope it is legitimate."

> *What would Fred have thought about my searching for this lost child again? He would have supported me. We did that for each other.*

"Good idea. I am super-tired; I'm a head to bed."

"Now? No dinner? But have some extra water before you lie down. All right?"

"Okay, I will."

FRED

FRED

My Zoe says she is wrinkled, gnarled, and likely melting. I say she is handsomely furrowed. Wise too, and generous. She got old but she couldn't help it. Me too.

Oh, I'm Fred, by the way.

Words are less my thing, although I love the way Indian languages mix in bits of English phrases, like salt. I leave words mostly to Zoe though. She says verbs are 30% of English words and 70% of some Native American languages. I wonder what that implies? More action, I suppose. Maybe more reflection. Faith is a verb—live our faith; show it in our deeds.

Me? I love plants. My teachers. I learned that if a plant is an "it," we can easily get a saw. If a plant is a "her," we think twice. The Indian way. In school, I learned the plant names; on the rez, the plants teach me their songs when I get down on one knee to feel them.

I love water and wind. My teachers. I learned that they know no boundaries; they shouldn't be bought or sold. What does this say about nationalism and political boundaries? Artificial. Unnatural.

Teachers are not only their words; they are their willingness to practice well what they teach. You know, we don't decide on the kind of profession we want, but on the kind of person we want to be. Agriculture on the rez with those kids, growing The Three Sisters. Hands in the dirt. That's me. Come fall, I'd see women carrying those Sisters' bushels of squash, corn, and beans on one hip and a baby on the other without hardly trying. My natural way is to see relationships; ways the world connects, not divides. Humans are not in charge of the world; we sometimes forget we are shaped by the same forces as all of life.

I mean, for example, how much has human-caused climate change been a part of accelerating -- even causing -- this global pandemic? A rhetorical question because the answer is obvious.

Working with the elders, I help the children rediscover traditions, expertise, and native roots, literally. Too much is being lost. I, in turn, learn from the elders about ancient eagle-trapping pits, holes topped with latticework covered with grasses and tethered rabbits, large enough for a man to hide in and pull the feathers from the eagle who lands, eager for the prey. It is a way to obtain eagle feathers for fans, plume arrows, or war bonnets. Without hurting the bird, of course.

And buffalo jumps. Cliffs where whole bison herds were driven, breaking their legs in the fall so they became easy prey. Their bodies were used for food—like pemmican—a greasy beef jerky—clothing, shelter, tools, bowstrings, laces, glue, and hides to tan. No waste. In hard years, some Indians now sell the ancient, sunbaked bison bones to dealers, to get food for their families. Sadly, some have even sold their reservation homes to non-Indians. To survive.

I suppose this is more than you wanted to know about me. Oh, well...

I hated that my people became needy by decree. I help families work through their nations' loss of fertile land to flooding from Army Corps of Engineer's river-damming—what they call *The Flood* in almost Biblical terms—that undermined agriculture. Check out Lawson's book, *Damned Indians*, if you want to see the scope of this pattern across reservation after reservation! I hate seeing the government slip in to try to *solve these Indians*, allowing the horrific environmental stress from fracking-fluid extraction of oil and gas, a roar like being three feet away from a gas-powered lawnmower, day in, day out, night in, night out. I do get too involved in these kinds of problems; I admit.

Using university connections, I stepped up to ensure the family burial areas were protected, knowing the ways they were connected to the way-back people. Sometimes the dead had been tenderly wrapped in bark and fixed high in a tree. Rather than being eaten by worms, their bodies would be eaten by raw-boned crows or vultures, then strewn over the earth rather than under. Maybe I will go like this someday. Different than African Americans, where a family will purchase a burial plot (in the part of a cemetery that doesn't have racial exclusions), even before they will buy a home.

I love my hands-on work. All of it. This is me. Yes, I do have some distant indigenous blood, but not enough to be an enrolled member in one of the 574 federally recognized tribes. Families ask me about this. My quiet ways and my respectful silence allow trust to grow in a world where distrust is too often a cynical expectation. There have been times I've visited a family in their home and we do not talk at all for the first hour. We just are. I know enough to understand that my people have walked a different road and breathed a different air.

I have a strong-scented memory of watching a toothless elder roll out pie dough on her kitchen table. Again, no words. No need even for verbs. She shook some flour onto the patterned oilcloth, kneaded the dough she had made earlier, and then patted it out with flour-covered hands. It fit perfectly in the dull and dented pie tin. She handed me a knife and some apples. We sat in silence, paring, cutting. The calm lay between us, smooth like still water. I know how to be in the quiet. Sometimes I can hear the tall grasses rubbing together in the wind; grass songs. Sometimes I see dust from a pickup racing by on the scoria road three hills over.

Trusted, I was included in sweat lodge ceremonies, overheated sage encrusted air burning my lungs. And pow wows, not orchestrated for tourists, that lasted through the cool night, elders honored with front row seats and flag-carrying veterans, beribboned fatigues heavy with battle metals, parading, solemnly. I was honored once, given a cherished painting. Trucks parked catawampus, blocking any exits. No one leaves early. No one wants to.

Funny story. Some kids and I planted a Three Sisters Garden in a vacant lot near the town square. We adapted Iroquois guidelines. Tribal elders sat silently watching us plant twelve mounds in a square. Weeks later, come harvest time, the elders returned, sitting on a nearby log, smoking and nodding in the late summer heat. Watching us.

The kids were trying to harvest beans and corn at the center of the dense mounds. They were getting scratched by the sharp-edged leaves as they reached into the mazes.

The rheumy-eyed elders knowingly smiled. Finally, the kids asked why.

"Why are you smiling?"

"It is better to have single or double rows of mounds to get to the crops from the sides."

"Why didn't you tell us that?"

The smiling elders quietly answered, "You didn't ask."

* * *

Sometimes people wondered why Zoe and I lived so far apart. I'd explain that the distance strengthened our love.

"Do you have children?" They would ask.

"We decided not to bring more children onto an overpopulated planet that can't support the people who are already alive," I'd say.

That was my standard answer to co-workers and it is mostly true, except for that one baby. I knew her history, but Zoe and I did not talk much about that long ago time or her son's adoption.

With the Covid, both of our colleges were in financial trouble. It is difficult to teach agriculture at a distance through Zoom and besides, the Internet connections were limited. Interruptible and sporadic, when they existed at all.

My administration encouraged me to retire. Zoe too, at her institution.

She and I agreed to take the buy-outs and finally try living together. But I got the Covid and then discovered thirty years hadn't been enough.

Cast my ashes on the rez.

Because the owl has called my name.

PREGNANT AND ALONE?

You ready to go to Dr. Foster's office? Remember to bring that mask."

During Covid, these necessary services, formerly delivered so smoothly that we mostly took them for granted, unraveled. Plowed roads. Clean parks. Access to fresh food and more. Top-notch healthcare for many. True, not everything needed to be convenient or easy all the time, but it felt like Covid moved us out of our predictable First World space.

> *I have Ruby Blue with me now. This is turning into a gift. I wonder what Fred would have thought about my current situation? He would have understood the underlying history for me, at least. And he knew about things like economic poverty so was more worldly than I am with my books.*

"Oh, shit. Where is that mask? Do we have to go today? I don't feel good."

"Yes, we have to go. Want to get an ice cream cone after?"

"I am not a child." Ruby Blue stomps her foot to slide it into her shoe, which is somewhat tight from her swollen ankles.

"Well, I'm not a child either but I love ice cream!"

A deep frown. Head turned to the side, slowly moving back and forth. Lips pursed. Jaw offended. "Zoe, I just want to be left alone."

"Sorry, not happening."

"You are not my mama. They are just gonna hurt me. Why hasn't Marcus called? Or written?"

"I know. I know. I'm sorry. Let's go; no protests there today."

* * *

The women call the clinic phone number from the parking lot and are told they may come in. They walk together, arm in arm, because Ruby Blue is feeling weak.

"Hi, hon." After the usual Covid questions, the ample nurse asks, "Is your baby-daddy in the picture?"

Zoe cringes, knowing what this continuing question means to Ruby Blue, whose face shows her frustration.

> *Why do y'all keep askin' me that shit! Yes, the father of my child is in the picture. I got more home trainin' than that.*

Ruby Blue flares. "Why did you ask that? I don't get it. Would you have said the same thing to a White woman?"

"Sorry, I didn't mean...I meant he could have come in with you."

"I know you didn't mean. THAT'S the problem." Ruby Blue turns away from the nurse.

Zoe interrupts, "How about if I come in today? This is a difficult time with the baby's birth getting closer and all the pressures."

"Sorry, we don't allow anyone to come in except the patient, and sometimes the father."

Shaking her head and blinking away her tears, Zoe states, "I will be right here outside. Maybe we will get that ice cream then."

* * *

Thirty minutes later, Ruby Blue comes out of the clinic door, crying. Zoe walks from the car to the clinic, glad that there are few cars in the parking lot with Covid limitations.

"She says I have fetal growth restriction and they may induce labor or I might have to have a C-section. What does this mean? That doctor is just gap-toothed trash. Don't go bonkers—just tell me."

Zoe offers a supportive arm, "This is difficult. Being pregnant and alone, without your man, is hard."

"I ain't got no good sense getting into this situation. And where is Marcus? Locked up. I should have just stuck to my own kind."

The women get in the car and Zoe starts the silent hybrid engine.

Leaning closer, "You did, Ruby Blue. You stuck to the human-kind. We are in this together, you and I. Remember that breathing we practiced? Sometimes we accept help and surrender." Then, cajoling, "And sometimes we have ice cream, like now."

Ruby Blue is slowly calming, yet still visibly annoyed, her arms crossed, resting high over the shelf of her pregnant stomach. A sigh, "I guess I could go for some cookies 'n cream."

Then, as Zoe turns into the empty street thinking about how easy driving is these days, "Zoe, they wanted to know if I have tattoos and what gangs I am affiliated with. Why do they think it is acceptable to ask questions like that? Don't they think of me as human? Who do they think they are? I'm so livid! You know what I'm sayin'!?"

"Don't cry, honey. I'm here with you. We are going to do this for you and Marcus and that tiny, beautiful child."

* * *

After getting ice cream—no cookies 'n cream was available but there was vanilla—Zoe calls Dr. Foster's office and is told what she already knew. Ruby Blue is having some depressive thoughts and anxiety. Dr. Foster explains, "She has a sense of hopelessness and fear for the future. Fatigue. Part of it is the pandemic stresses and part of it is her elevated-risk pregnancy. Keep her as calm as you can, continue the diet, and focus on bed rest. We are trying to avoid a pre-term C-section, so need to allow her body to prepare for vaginal birth if possible. Being Black, young, first pregnancy, and having a family-history of this high-blood pressure disorder all contribute to her risk. And trauma from the pandemic and police/protest violence is actually leading to some preterm and underweight babies."

* * *

With attempted cheerfulness, Zoe suggests, "Let's have you lie on the couch this evening and we will watch some TV. We have Netflix now, so we can see more movies. The news is all about the Covid pandemic—too much slanted political affirmation, not always information. Let's skip that, although there was a sweet story—a positive story on TV—of a woman who gave birth while she was sick with Covid but then got to see her newborn baby today for the first time with a live video from the hospital. A positive outcome for everyone. Anyway, what is your favorite movie?"

With an unrushed response, Ruby Blue proposes, "How about *The Nutty Professor*? Seems about right with the doc all worried about me gainin' weight. And you with your ice cream! I like Eddie Murphy and Jada Pinkett Smith."

A long sigh, then, "You know, we Black women have to be strong. We cannot show weakness or outrage without seeming threatening. I was mad at the questions the doctor's office people asked me today. How do I express that? I bring my whole self to this situation. My body, my history, my fear, my fury, my oppression, and even my humor. True that. And then they see even my questions as angry when I'm feelin' hurt or misunderstood. No one asks about my real feelings. How do I hold anger and sadness inside of me at the same time? Do we just have to tend to our own selves? I guess, at some point, you need to decide for yourself who you gonna be. I want to harness this rage. But how?"

Picking up the Fire Stick she won at a college faculty meeting on technology updates and preparing to ask the device to locate the movie, Zoe pauses. "As always, you make such very good points. The big questions. I think we need to confront our deepest wounds first, as you are helping me do with that adoption of my son. Really confront and learn how to hold that pain and sadness and fury all at the same time. To understand more deeply. I believe that people are fundamentally good, which may well, as I think about it, be part of my lifelong White privilege, or maybe economic privilege. What do you think?"

Waiting for Zoe, determined to call up *The Nutty Professor* with a voice command, Ruby Blue asks, "What does it feel like to be White? Do you think I'd enjoy being White?"

Directing the Fire Stick like a classroom pointer, Zoe muses. "That is a hard question. I was unaware of my Whiteness until Fred began to teach me through his experiences on the reservation. I think the central point about being White is that I never had to consider it. Race was not an issue in any parts of my life. Nothing about other people's racial struggles truly impacted my day-to-day world. I mean, I could listen to the news, or a person's personal story of hurt, and then return to my ordinary, predictable life.

"Another Black man shot? Too bad. How awful." But-such cruelties—like the killings—are so remote from my life. And I always had no idea what to do. How could anything I would do make a difference? Fred taught me some. You have opened my eyes much further. I now see at least some of how racism and inequities continue to hurt us all. For Whites like me, it is a fake crown too many of us believe we deserve."

Zoe pauses, still fussing with the TV remote control, then continues, "I remember the announcement when the human genome was fully mapped, about the turn of the century, showing that all humans were 99.9 percent the same, and we all migrated out of Africa. Imagine! Many do not realize this but perhaps it is becoming clearer as we move toward the day, in your lifetime, when the U.S. will be "majority minority" as they say. By 2042, I'm remembering. And I've seen minority White populations in many of the countries I've traveled to, like South Africa. I also see that it is going to take all of us, pushing against the system as it exists, to embrace these inevitable changes. You, Marcus, me, the baby. All of us."

Zoe hands the remote control to Ruby Blue, knowing she was born knowing how to use it. Ruby Blue nods, but does not add anything to Zoe's monologue. She is glad to have the security and relative ease she and Zoe have built. Glad to have this safety while she is feeling vulnerable with the confusing pregnancy and her growing apprehensions.

Sitting in her chair and waiting for the movie to stop buffering, "Ruby Blue, you are teaching me, and reminding me perhaps, that doing nothing is not an option. Even as an olding woman, I cannot just relax and allow the world to pass me by, easy as that could be, especially in this global epidemic. I have more than enough.

"*What* and *how* are the big questions. What are we going to do differently? How much history should be reconsidered? There was Michigan Representative John Conyers' H.R. 40 reparation proposal that he introduced in the legislature, yearly, for almost 30 years. He tried to address the *how*: *how* to deal with the current impacts of historical actions, the legacy of slavery.

"His proposal has not been addressed.

"And then I wonder how many people really want radical change (which seems to be linked, these days, with fundamentalisms or irrational passions) and how do we teach more? I remember a quote from Mother Teresa, 'Not all of us can do great things but we can do small things with great love.'

"But we are supposed to be relaxing tonight. Enough ranting. *The Nutty Professor*, here we come! My first time seeing this movie!"

As the TV continues searching for the movie, Zoe ponders.

> *How is it that I know (and have taught) facts about*
> *reparations and racism and inequities, but have never*

stood up to work toward change? I mean, truly put myself on the line? Even with Fred being on the reservation, I was able to see the inequities first-hand, but again, always back to the safety and security of my own little world. What does that say about me as a human being? What does it imply about the authenticity of what I espouse?

As the movie credits appear on the screen, "Really? This is your first time watchin' *The Nutty Professor?*" Ruby Blue's shoulders visibly relax. "You are goin' to be a mighty happy woman. Eddie Murphy plays nearly all the parts. Maybe after the baby comes, I'll do some of those exercises he tries out. But maybe not the acupuncture scene. Have you ever tried it?"

"Yes, I have. It was relaxing and probably worked," Zoe nods as her facial muscles release into a full and unencumbered smile.

The movie rings out to *Macho Man* pulsing, body builders dancing, and Professor Klumps—aka Eddie Murphy—fine tuning his professional look.

VOICE MAIL

After refreshing her memories of the Nutty Professor's dietary and personality transformation into Buddy Love, Ruby Blue shuffles off to bed, still smiling at the silliness of the film. It has lifted her mood.

Zoe begins putting away clean dishes from the dish rack and sees a flickering light on the phone, wondering how long there has been a voice message. She lifts the receiver and dials her number, then presses the star key, pausing, then entering the mailbox pin. With so few calls since Fred's death, she has to focus on the process. She has nearly forgotten how to retrieve voice mail.

Listening through the receiver, she stands. Stunned. Mouth agape, then putting one finger over her lips as if to erase or silence the message, she listens to the words that come as if in slow motion; the way people say they experience an accident. She can barely breathe. She shakes her head. Tears bleed down her cheeks.

"No. No. NO!" Aloud.

She repeats the retrieval process, listening again, thinking she must have heard wrong.

> *This cannot be. This cannot happen. What do I do?*
> *What to do? Fred, what should I do? I have to tell her,*
> *but I do not want to. But I have to. She isn't well*
> *enough to hear this. Her blood pressure. Who can I call?*
> *Her physician, Dr. Foster? Her caseworker, Eleanor?*

Only professional friends. There is no family; no other people. Only me.

Zoe accesses the voice mail a third time.

No. No. This can't be…

She dials Dr. Foster's number, even though it is late. A message tells her to call the hospital if this is an emergency, then begins wading through all the Covid questions about shortness of breath and fever and coughs. Zoe leaves a brief message, then hangs up.

> *I have to take her to the hospital before I tell her. She needs to hear this where she is safe and can receive the medical care she will likely need. Wait. Wait. There isn't any real urgency. Done is done. Tomorrow. We will go to the hospital in the morning.*

Zoe sits, staring at the phone. Just staring. Her hands shaking, wringing fist over fist. She finally moves to the living room and lies on the couch, fully dressed, covering herself with the crocheted blanket that has so long been a fixture there. Of course, sleep won't come. Her mind is spinning. But exhaustion eventually quiets her, even though there is no real rest in it.

BIRTHING

Zoe! Wake your ass up. Why did you sleep on the couch? What's wrong?"

Zoe stirs, feeling drugged, then remembers. "Ruby Blue. Ruby Blue."

Sitting on the edge of the couch and reaching for Zoe's hand, "What? You are scaring me. What is wrong?" Ruby Blue asks.

"We need to get some water for you, and something to eat. Then we are going to the hospital," Zoe blurts out.

"Why? What is going on? Are you okay?"

"No, I'm not okay." Zoe is telling the truth. "We need to go very soon."

"I'll get our coats. Can you drive?"

"Yes. It isn't far and I'm okay to drive. Drink some water."

* * *

Zoe parks in the hospital Emergency entrance, ignoring the Covid instructions. The women, wearing their masks, walk arm in arm toward the automatic door, violating yet more Covid rules as they enter without having pre-approval.

A triage nurse in protective gear rushes up to them and Zoe demands, "Page Dr. Foster. It is a pregnancy emergency."

What is happening? Why won't she tell me anything? Is she having a heart attack? Stroke? I don't know what to do. I need you. We need you. Ol' lady, you better not die on me.

Silent, they sit together on the orange plastic chairs. Dr. Foster quickly enters the room, then, with the doctor listening, Zoe turns to Ruby Blue and places wrinkled hands on both of the younger woman's cheeks, a loose, wire-thin band of gold shifting on her cold ring finger.

"I don't know how to tell you this. I need you to breathe. Ruby Blue. He's dead. Marcus. He died in prison. I couldn't tell you at home. I was afraid for you and the baby. I had to tell you with Dr. Foster present."

Ruby Blue's cry echoes through the hospital. "*NOOOO!*" Her face flushes and she puts a hand on her left chest, then vomits. She is gasping for air and leans down as best she can, knees wide, with the baby pressing.

Dr. Foster turns quickly and instructs the triage nurse to immediately bring a wheelchair. "We are going to admit her for a C-section. Now."

Sobbing. Confused. Frightened. Panicking, she blurts out, "Zoe, Zoe, Zoe, don't leave me. The baby and I get to stay with you, right? Nothin' is gonna change, right? You are still my foster person, right?" And my daughter's foster mom too, right?"

Reaching for her hand, Zoe reassures, "I'll never leave you. I'll be here as soon as they tell me I can pick you up, hon. You are going to be fine. You are a strong Black woman. You've got this."

The idea of being with her during the delivery may actually be more terrifying for me than it is for her. But if allowed, I could do it. I could do this if I needed to.

For Ruby Blue. But Covid doesn't allow me to be with her. A relief actually, if I'm completely honest.

After Ruby Blue is wheeled away, her sobs echoing down the hallway, the compassionate nurse asks Zoe to leave the hospital immediately. They both know she can't stay and that rules have already been bent. "Don't worry. She is in good hands with Dr. Foster."

Zoe returns home to the stillness. Hollowness. Once again, she retrieves the phone message.

"This is Lieutenant Myer from the Middleborough Prison. It is imperative that you contact the facility as soon as possible. We have used all reasonable means to find Marcus' family through our records, without success. Your name appeared in the phone accounts or other communication. We have information relative to your boyfriend's demise.

Initial findings show his death was caused by Covid-19 pneumonia. Root cause evidence collection has proceeded according to protocol and an administrative investigation will follow adhering to prison policies, including disciplinary action, if called for. His remains have been released to a mortuary and since they were not claimed within 48 hours, disposition was made as provided by law. We're deeply sorry, ma'am, and extend sympathy for your loss."

How could this happen? How could a young man die? How dare they inform us with a voice message? Truly the world is broken. Covid has broken so much.

* * *

The phone rings. Zoe is startled awake from her doze—or is it full exhaustion?—head lying on her arm bent and resting on the kitchen table. The harsh sound is startling and she cannot immediately remember why she is feeling so distraught.

Oh, Marcus' death. And the C-section.

Answering the call. "Yes."

"Zoe? It is Dr. Foster. The C-section—a usual low transverse incision—went well and both Ruby and her daughter are doing fine. I have given Ruby light sedation for the time being. The surgery, coupled with her husband's death, is just too much. But I'm pleased to say that her blood pressure is actually lower and seems to be controlled. Her daughter is in the NICU, in a radiant warmer, just to stabilize her body temperature. But she is doing very well and won't be there long. Both of them will be in the hospital now for several days. You will be able to talk with Ruby by phone. But not yet. And, obviously, no visiting.

"Preeclampsia is such an oddity and researchers don't understand why a disease that can damage both mother and baby has survived. You'd think natural selection would have, literally, killed it off. But the baby is fine, Apgar score of eight. She is active..."

Zoe starts to feel warm, breaking into a smile.

So, Ruby Blue was right about having a daughter. I should have known she knew what she was feeling.

Dr. Foster asks, "Zoe, are you still there? Did you hear me? The baby is breathing well, has a strong pulse, and good color.

"Oddly, some medical texts still tell us to look for pink color in a healthy newborn, which doesn't always work for babies of color. But I know what healthy looks like and this girl is well and strong. For Ruby, she needs to know that she is at a slightly, and I mean slightly, if monitored, risk of some heart problems or type-2 diabetes when she is older. If she gets pregnant again, she needs to know she may also develop preeclampsia with that pregnancy. She doesn't need to be afraid of that, just aware. And, she is returning to your house, right?"

"Yes, I will remind her of these things and thank you, Dr. Foster. Thank you for your quick response."

"It was good that you brought her to the hospital when you did."

NATIONAL ADOPTION REGISTRY

The mailbox on the front of the house clanks shut and Zoe responds to the familiar sound as she has for decades.

Bills and advertisements. That is all the mail I get these days. But it is a link with the outside world. So, should I wash off the mail or leave it outside for three days? Covid germs? Guess I'll risk it! It is sounding more and more like the main Covid dangers are airborne and not passed so much through touch. Besides, the mail person wears gloves. All of this is more than I want to spend my time thinking about right now with Ruby Blue and the baby. Truly.

Slipped between the junk mail is a letter from the National Adoption Registry, the organization Zoe wrote to asking for information on the son she gave birth to and then let go for adoption. It had been Ruby Blue's idea to do that, to pursue finding out what had happened to the baby.

Dear Ms. Smyth.

We have located the records on your son, born 6-18-63 in San Antonio. Texas Cradle no longer exists, but the records were transferred to the state. As happens in so many birth records from that era, both the name you gave him, David, and the date of his birth were modified. His adoptive parents' names are listed as his biological parents, but they never completed the adoption.

I am so very sorry to tell you that David did not survive. He was boarded with a foster family right after birth. We do not have access to the cause of death, but do know that he died before moving in with his new family. Although we now offer DNA services to increase the chances of finding family members, we assume that will not help you in this instance.

We send our deepest condolences.
Sincerely,
National Adoption Registry

I do not know what to feel. Ruby Blue's baby alive. Mine dead. Ruby Blue alive and well. Fred and Marcus dead.

I need to find out what happened to Marcus, if not for my own curiosity, at least for Ruby Blue's sake.

"I CANNOT HELP YOU WITH THAT"

Zoe dials the prison phone number, hopeful of finding out something about what happened to Marcus.

A blunt, one-word response on the phone. "Security."

"I'm calling about the death of a prisoner."

"I cannot help you with that, Ma'am. Call Medical."

"Do you have the number?"

"I will transfer you."

The phone rings once, then disconnects. Zoe redials then opts for Medical Services from the phone tree.

"Health."

"I am calling about the death of a prisoner."

"I cannot help you with that, Ma'am. You need to call his social worker. What's his number? I need his ID to tell you which social worker."

"I just have his name. He was moved to your facility temporarily because of Covid quarantine in the jail and more space in the prison. He hadn't even been sentenced."

"I cannot help you."

"Transfer me to the warden. Please."

"I cannot do that."

Increasingly angry and frustrated, Zoe calls the prison phone tree for the fourth time and selects the listing for Administration.

"Warden's office. Please leave a message after the beep."

Why does the criminal justice system seem to feel it has to punish the families of the people it cares for? Is it this opaque when there is no Covid excuse? I wonder.

I'll call the hospital instead even though I have no new information for Ruby Blue, and try not to toss my frustration on her.

"Hi, Ruby Blue. How are you and your baby doing?"

"Every time they try to walk me, my head starts swirling and I come close to falling down, and you can't believe how much it hurts to move. They say I gotta. I'm chill, if I've got to, I have to. Walk it off. This ain't the time to be weak. My baby girl needs me to be strong so that's what I'm goin' to do."

"How beautiful is your daughter?"

"She's good but I'm distracted as all get out. Can't believe Marcus has passed. If I had family, they would show up to remember Marcus with lotions, proverbs, and patience, and the ability to cook for a home-going celebration. That's the way. Did you find out what happened?"

"I'm working on that."

My frustration is rising again, but there is no need to share that right now. No one seems to have answers. No one will tell me anything. I'll have to go higher up in the system and threaten in some ways. Hate this.

"We are tryin' to find a way for me to breastfeed her, which hurts. I lie on my side, which hurts. She lies on her side facing me so she isn't lying on my stitches, which hurts! I support her head then touch my breast to her lips. She is trying. I am trying. The nurse is trying to get her to latch, or so she says. We will get there, or so she says. I told her ass to stop wiggling—the baby, not the nurse."

This is the first bit of humor I've heard from her in many days; she isn't feeling like Eeyore right now: not sounding pessimistic, gloomy, or depressed, even with losing Marcus. I sense she is connecting with motherhood and this tiny child.

Zoe wonders, "What are you going to name her?"

"Marcus and I didn't finish anything, except some dreams. You know, it seems like God didn't decide to give the Black man nothin' but dreams. But now there is a child to make some of my visions seem worthwhile. At least I got her."

"And me, Ruby Blue. You've got me, too."

"That is good. We are going to try this breast feeding again now. Gotta go."

* * *

Zoe begins the search for information once again by dialing the state-level Department of Corrections number.

"Division of Adult Institutions."

"I'm calling about the death of a prisoner."

"What was his or her DOC number?"

"I just have his name. He was moved temporarily. He hadn't even been sentenced before he died. He was moved from the county jail to Middleborough Prison because of the Covid quarantine."

"I cannot help you, Ma'am. You need to call the county jail."

Fury growing again, "But he died in one of your institutions. I would like to speak to the administrator."

"I'll transfer you."

*"YOU HAVE REACHED THE MAIN NUMBER FOR
THE DEPARTMENT OF CORRECTIONS. REGULAR
BUSINESS HOURS ARE 8AM TO 4:30PM, MONDAY
THROUGH FRIDAY. FOR ADULT
INSTITUTIONS,*

*PLEASE PRESS ONE FOR RECORDS
RELATED TO COMMUNITY SUPERVISION,
PROBATION, OR PAROLE.*

*PLEASE PRESS TWO FOR MANAGEMENT
SERVICES.*

*PLEASE PRESS THREE FOR COMMUNITY
CORRECTIONS, INCLUDING SEX OFFENDER
REGISTRATION.*

*PLEASE PRESS FOUR FOR JUVENILE
CORRECTIONS.*

*PLEASE PRESS FIVE FOR THE OFFICE OF
VICTIM SERVICES.*

*PLEASE PRESS SIX FOR THE OFFICE OF
PRISON RAPE ELIMINATION.*

*PLEASE PRESS SEVEN FOR ALL OTHER
SERVICES.*

PLEASE PRESS EIGHT ..."

*Why did I listen through those options? Was I expecting
to press nine for death of a prisoner?*

Zoe presses eight.

*This is Dante's first circle of Hell. Limbo. Not the limbo
of being unbaptized, but the limbo of awaiting a
resolution. I wonder if she will want to baptize her
daughter. We haven't talked about religion. I don't*

230

sense that it is central to her life, but maybe was with her grandmother, as she talks about that woman who was special in her young life.

"Please wait while I transfer your call." Then, "All of our staff are busy helping other people. Please leave a message at the tone."

"This is Dr. Zoe Smyth. I am the foster parent to Ruby Smith, fiancée of a prisoner who died in your custody just over 48 hours ago. His body was cremated before we got notice. He had been transferred from the County Jail to Middleborough Prison because of Covid quarantine. He never had a hearing or received a sentence. We need to know what happened to him. I am leaving my phone number and address for you to respond. If we do not hear back within a week, I will contact a lawyer and file a Request for Public Records through the Department of Justice."

Zoe's hand shakes as she hangs up, with more force than would be needed to rest the yellow phone on the wall receiver. The long cord tangles below, curling to the floor.

A SINGLE MOM

Wait. I just realized a baby—A BABYYY—is moving in with us. A baby! We weren't ready for this. I wasn't ready for this. Real, this is real. We need some things, but what? Thank goodness for the Internet.

What? Wait? Wrong site. I don't want to know about all the colors and textures of a baby's poop. I want to know what are the basics I need to order for her. I'd better call the hospital again.

Ruby Blue. We need to order some things for your baby. But what?"

Ruby Blue's smile is evident even through the phone line. "Well, something to wear. A blanket to be warm. It is more about what she doesn't need, like shoes. Yet. We ain't gonna go nowhere. Don't need a fancy bed; she can sleep in the drawer in my bedroom. Maybe somethin' for you to carry her in because they tell me I can't be liftin' with the C-section."

Now Zoe can hear Ruby Blue's voice cracking with new emotion, "I'm gonna try my hardest to make her happy and teach her all about her daddy. He was a fine man—good and fair—just couldn't never catch up with his dreams. He won't ever be sending her a birthday card. Seems it is too easy to die."

232

Not wanting to talk about death right now when the topic is new life, Zoe tells herself,

> *We're kind of a mess. Two women grieving the loss of the men in our lives. And then the information on my baby given up for adoption too. We can't let sadness take over. Postpartum depression? I need to read up on this rather than on baby feces. Maybe talk with Dr. Foster more. But she is so busy; so stretched with the Covid ordeal.*

"Okay, I'll order the things I think we need for you two to come home. I'll figure it out for us, okay? Do you like pink?"

"Yes, bright pink. I want my baby to shine like her daddy. Her skin is the color of coffee, of course, and she's got curls. She moves just like she did inside of me. It is like I already know her. The nurses say C-section babies are the prettiest with their round heads. I've gotta think about a name for her."

Ruby Blue's voice is drifting off. Fatigue, maybe. Pain medication, maybe.

"Do you know when you can come home?"

"I have some little contractions goin' on, so we are waitin' to see about that. And bleeding. They told me I can't have sex for several weeks. I laughed and told them to just let me alone. Ain't none of that happenin' in my life anytime soon. But I know they don't mean nothin' by it; they just don't know. They just doin' they job."

"Get some rest, hon. I wish I could be there to hold you both. But I can tell you are strong and doing so, so well. Wonder woman!"

"Bye."

MARCA HOPE SMITH

Ruby Blue slides her baby, now wrapped in a pink onesie, across the sheet, closer to her side, then sniffs her head, her curls. She runs a hand down the baby's leg, feeling the soft swell of thigh, calf, and miniature foot, exploring this perfect tiny human, and then lets a flawless fist grab her finger. Tightly. She kisses the baby's head. Who is she? Who is she gonna be? The baby looks at her intently; they stare at each other, silently asking, *Hey there, what are you?* Neither of them is sure.

Yes, we have a child, Marcus. Hey, baby. Who are you? Speak your name. It isn't Zoe; it might be Marcus. Well, not Marcus but how about Marca? You are the positive hope of my life. Hope. How about Marca Hope Smith. Okay, that will work. I'm laughing 'cause yo hair is on point girl, but then so is mine. We are connected that way.

No words from you? Well, you don't have to talk until you are good and ready. And then what will you say? Love you. Mom? And what will I say? Come here baby girl, let me shake some sense into you? Naw. I'm going to be the best, most loving mom you ever had. Well, no competition, I guess, since I will be the only mom you ever get. Your grandma, Zoe, and I will be the best. You will give us new meaning. Somethin' for us to continue getting' out of bed for. You will be the reason why we continue the fight.

JUST ANOTHER COVID CASUALTY

Zoe answers the phone, thinking it will be Ruby Blue calling with details on what to purchase for the baby's homecoming.

"Ma'am, I'm the prison chaplain at Middleborough Prison, responding to your voice message. Marcus tested positive for Covid-19 after he was transferred from the County Jail. Like so many inmates, he did not trust the medics here, so did not ask for help."

"So, let me get this straight. You're telling me it was his fault he died? You can't be serious!" Zoe feels her anger rising.

"Prison walls are porous with officers and employees going in and out every day. There is just more exposure on the inside, and over-crowding adds to the risk. We don't have the staff we need and, yes, there are guys who are sick but not being treated for Covid.

"Our priority during this public health crisis is the safety and health of DOC staff and persons in our care. We have taken many steps to keep Covid-19 out of our institutions and limit the spread of the virus at facilities with positive cases. Health Services staff at DOC institutions, in collaboration with local health departments and the State Department of Health Services, are diligently working to meet the medical needs of persons in our care who contract this virus."

Angry, Zoe yells, "I CANNOT BELIEVE you are just reading these random dispassionate words to me! What do I tell his fiancée and his day-old daughter? Do I say he died because he ignored being tested and because you have limited and porous staff? I am so very angry about this. You killed Marcus!"

"We are very sorry for your loss, Ma'am."

"You don't say. Yes, me too. Me too. Is there a prison video that records injury and death situations? Did he die in his cell? What about a cellmate? Was he sick too?"

"I don't know, Ma'am. The prison video system regularly overrides automatically. So, no record. But we will mail you his belongings. We are sorry for your loss, Ma'am."

Click.

THE PINK HEADBAND

Zoe is fuming. Sputtering to herself about the phone call.

What can I tell her? What the hell am I supposed to tell her! Fred, what? The system likely did kill Marcus, but does she need to carry that knowledge with her for the rest of her life? To what degree do I intervene and protect this vulnerable young woman, who may actually be tougher than I am. What are the boundaries for a parent? Well, a foster parent in this case. A foster grandmother. Yikes, I'm a grandmother! Fred, we are grandparents.

The phone rings again.

Is this the chaplain calling back with more information and maybe an authentic apology? No, this time it is Ruby Blue.

"Zoe, they are tellin' me we get to go home day after tomorrow if everything stays good. My incision is healing well, not red or swollen or leaking. One minute I'm cryin' and the next, holdin' my daughter. Minute after, I am afraid, then wakin' up. I feel safer at your—no, our—house. I will be better, the nurses tell me. I've named her. *Marca Hope Smith.* What do you think? She named after Marcus, and the hope we have for the future. I'll need to add hope and Marca Hope to our Vision Board."

"Yes, for sure and I love your name choice."

"Wait, Zoe, have you heard anything from the prison?"

"Yes, Marcus died from the monster Covid virus. He was probably already sick when they moved him from the County Jail, and quickly got sicker in the prison. Correctional officers are not trained in infection control, they told me. By the time they realized how ill he really was, there was nothing they could do to save him. The prison simply did not have acute care equipment in their infirmary to treat him and it was already full of ailing inmates anyway. We have seen the images on the news night after night. So many people who are so very ill. Marcus was too sick before they could even move him to the local hospital, to a ventilator. There were National Guard medics present, but it was pneumonia that ultimately took him. He was sedated, so he did not suffer."

Silence, then Ruby Blue quietly sobs, "Guess we are all born to die."

"And a part of you dies when a loved one dies. Losing Fred has taught me that. He comes to me often and is there when I have questions. He helps me. I think Marcus will help you with Marca too."

Speaking in almost a whisper, Ruby Blue sighs, "There is no one left who knew Marcus except me. He doesn't exist in the memory of anyone who is living, well, other than those people in the prison, and maybe in the jail, and those thieves who took my stimulus money. I don't care if any of those people remember him. But I need to tell Marca about him. I will tell her. I'll tell these nurses too. I am getting' a lot of love."

There is a softening in Ruby Blue's voice. A settling. A sense of comfort.

"I'm glad that the nurses are being kind. They are dealing with unrelenting stress from this virus, so having a new life may be the best thing that has happened to them in a while. You and Marca are bringing joy to people, including me. But now I need to order some baby things for us to have for when you come home. There is just a lot, lot to do!"

Amazon.com: Baby girl newborn essentials.

> *Yes, this seems like what we need. Sleeper. Bib. Infant swaddle blanket. Burp cloth. Pacifier. Newborn diapers —cloth ones. This stuff is all expensive. And there is a bright pink head band, just like Marcus would want for his baby girl. If it were not for Covid, we could get some of it second-hand. Marca Hope will grow fast, I expect. Car seats—$100! Well, maybe we can just get them home first and then make these other decisions. We will have the foster parent money soon and Ruby Blue will know what she wants.*

> *Fred, I'm feeling bewildered. Death and life. I won't go to the Internet to figure this out because I don't need platitudes even though I expect a lot of people are experiencing their own versions of this same mix of joy and profound grief and frustration, all braided together in the same breath.*

> *Humanity. I suppose this mixture can happen because I am merely human. Does the grief of losing you, and even Marcus though I never got to meet him, enable me to experience life more abundantly? To live more fully? Perhaps to love more intensely?*

> *Before she came, I was just being. Missing you, trying to read my books, watching TV, and thinking about*

getting a cat. Now, look at what my life has become because I invited serendipity in. I am both a human being and, progressively, a human doing! A whirlwind. A new version of living even when I don't have all that much time left on this earth. I am becoming the fila-ment that unites a small pool of diverse people together.

Maybe I'm not doing great things, but as Mother Teresa offered, I am doing small things with growing love. I wish you were here to help, to listen, and to savor all of this with me...wait, you are here. More so than if you were stuffed and sitting on the couch as we once teased! Miss you, Fred. Love you.

Perhaps a little Merlot for the quiet evening that may be my last for a while. Yep.

#COMINGHOME

W hy are you tryin' to deny me?" Ruby Blue teases. "It is breakin' warm outside. Now we are seein' the sun. It is that day when the temperatures inside and outside are the same. Spring."

Zoe looks out of the kitchen window, past the African violet resting in its usual spot on the windowsill.

> *It is time to rake the flowerbed leaves and stems into a pile from where they have scattered and drifted over winter. Love those unique odors from the belly of spring. Dry plants on top and, most years, wet underneath from the last of the winter moisture. No leaf burning here even though there is not a nearby neighbor. Healthy mulch rather than particulates, hydrocarbons, and carbon monoxide, as Fred would remind me. Yearly.*

"Just a few more days of recovering from this C-section, this major surgery. And your body is recuperating from being pregnant too. Dr. Foster has given us our 'walking papers.' Our 'Rules of the Road.' No lifting things heavier than Marca Hope. And I'll continue making our preeclampsia diet. Good for us both. Soon the three of us will be walking daily."

"My breasts are all swollen. They hurt. Warm washcloths before breast feedin', cool after, the nurse said. And my hair is falling out big time. It's hard to manage when it's—well, raw. I need it to be braided neatly."

"Yes, the postpartum information talks about hair loss and then those stretch marks that won't disappear, but will fade. And our walks will help lose any extra weight."

"I knnnooowww you ain't sayin' I'm fat! And I hate these extra-absorbent menstrual pads. The person who invented them must have never had to wear them!"

"You are good. We are good."

"Teasing you. Gimme some sugar."

The women hug, appreciating each other and feeling comfortable being back together.

"We are safe here. Marca is safe. Now if we just had Marcus. Things ain't the same since he passed. But I don't want this to be a sad fest. I need to physically let go. But I know he will be with us forever, spiritually. He was a fine man."

Nodding in agreement, Zoe adds, "We are both grieving and both loving, aren't we? They say that the risk of love is loss. Guess we know that, and know we will take the risk again."

"And you promised to make us some of your crooked food before Marca wakes up. I remember my grandmother's food. She made jelly so sweet it made you lick the jar. Maybe I'll cook for us down the road."

Ruby Blue smiles at her own joke, but also knows, no question, she is the better cook.

#THEADOPTION

As Zoe starts slicing carrots on the walnut cutting board Fred made for her one Christmas while thinking that it needs to be oiled again to preserve it, Ruby Blue gazes at Marca Hope, who is sleeping in the antique oak dresser drawer carefully lined with swaddling blankets and securely resting on the kitchen table. The women look at the baby, then turn and smile at each other, silently taking shared credit for the peaceful, healthy girl.

Putting her elbow on Zoe's shoulder, affectionately, the women tip their heads toward each other, toasting the moment. The quiet is easy. Comfortable. The new norm.

Almost shyly, Ruby Blue turns to Zoe. "I've been thinkin'."

Now standing next to the stove, distracted, Zoe continues dropping sliced carrots into boiling water, answering, "Yes, about what, hon?"

"Have you ever thought about adoption?"

Zoe lifts the wooden spoon she is stirring with and looks over at the sleeping baby. "Adoption? Yes, I thought about that when Vikisita followed me around the Indian orphanage for all those days, clearly wanting me to take her home. And I thought about it deeply, of course, after I realized what I had done, giving my son up to be adopted by a two-parent family. And now? That is such a kind thought, but I am just too old to adopt Marca."

"Marca?"

Ruby Blue pauses, considering the response, then whispers, "I meant me. Adopt me. I want you to adopt me."

Zoe turns further, lips slightly parted, wanting to read Ruby Blue's face, to see if she means what she has just said. Clearly it is an idea that hadn't crossed Zoe's mind before this moment. A pause; while waves of feelings run through her mind, and heart.

> *What would people say? Wait, what people? All our friends are dead or gone. What would "who" say? Wait, why would I care?*

"Adopt you? You? Adopt you? Hmm." Zoe lowers the heat on the stove, half smiles, turns toward the coffee pot, pours two cups, then places them on the table. Ruby Blue pours milk into each cup, adds a teaspoon of sugar, and stirs them with a shared spoon.

"Adopt you?" Zoe is turning this idea over and over, allowing it to settle into her brain like slow waves seeping into a pristine sandy shore.

Marca Hope stirs and Ruby Blue reaches into the drawer and touches her gently, soothing her, soothing both of them in the muted moment.

"And, of course, if you were to adopt me, you'd be adopting Marca Hope too."

"Marca Hope would be my granddaughter? More like great-granddaughter. You would be my granddaughter? Official. For real. Forever."

Laughing and looking down, awkwardly, Zoe ponders, out loud, "A two-parent family, connections across race, good housing and schools and access to healthcare and healthy food, doors to basic information, a mother in college as a role model. Do you want all of this for Marca Hope?"

Then answering her own question, Zoe states, "I do. Fred would. This could be the two of us, working together for her, and your, futures. A team. A pair. I don't want to imagine her future based only on what I think is best. Joint parenting and decision-making."

The women sit in silence, sipping their coffee, facing each other, thinking, Marca resting between them. Unconsciously, as always, Zoe runs her finger around the edge of the sugar bowl, pondering.

The words stretch out between them, hanging like fresh laundry on a soft, warm, breezy day.

Zoe continues, "Forever. You know, no one has ever offered me anything of this size, this potential scope. In my entire life. Never.

"I'm thinking about all of what we have been through in much less than one year, Ruby Blue. Even with our losses, Covid has been a gift for us, giving us profound time together. We built the best out of what could have been torture, and was, for millions of people. We have built memories. We have built trust. We have built a strong connection; an unbreakable bond. We have built love. I love you. I love Marca Hope."

Ruby Blue nods and silently mouths, "We love you too."

Zoe pauses, "Adoption? There are all sorts of implications, but as I think about this, they are all good. All positive. Adoption. Adopt you?" Zoe smiles. "Yes, adopt both of you. Lean on each other. My family. Your family. Our family.

"You realize this would mean you adopt me too? With all my idiosyncratic olding White ways? Suppose the dementia grabs hold of me? Suppose I have a stroke and tip over? Suppose, suppose, suppose."

"Yep. I get it that the future is unknown." Ruby Blue shifts her weight to her other hip on the hard kitchen chair, still not fully recovered from the surgery.

"Zoe, remember when I told you about watchin' your wrinkled hands stirring the batter for those sweet potato waffles that you burned to near unrecognizable when I first came to your house and you were trying to do something nice just for me? Remember the song by Bill Withers about his grandmother, a slave? She also had well-used hands that touched and worked. You used your hands—and your heart— to care for me in my hardest moments. You were there for me even though it was painful for you to go through a difficult pregnancy, given your memories. You did not step away. You stayed. Just like you promised you would. You have been here for me and Marca Hope, even when we lost Marcus. No one else has ever done that for me. No one. We want to be here for you."

Zoe reaches over with a long, hard sideways hug, and a kiss on the cheek.

Marca Hope fusses, opening her eyes. She turns, sees the women looking down at her, and offers a series of baby coos and tuts and clucks. Contentment. Safety.

A little child shall lead them.

"Yes. Adoption. A chosen family."

#ZOE MUSINGS

How life has changed in just these few months.

I continue to grieve the losses of Fred and Marcus, but am learning to hold the sorrow softly.

I grieve as well for the traumas experienced by Ruby Blue's and my ancestors that we still carry—often veiled, even baffling—into our everyday perceptions.

At the same time, I am remade. I have never felt loves like I now embrace. Yes, I loved Fred as a partner and husband. And I loved my students for their curiosity, engagement, and youthful delight.

Now, two gentle, caring hands are laced together. Ruby Blue's and mine.

Now, a tiny brown finger entwines around mine. Tightly. Hungrily. Trustingly.

Now, we share sounds of happiness and wonder, like a clutch of interlaced and purring kittens, suckling.

Maybe we three can do this. Maybe this is enough. More than enough. Beyond my (yes, beloved) book pages and scholarly experiences, there is a new level of living. I did not know.

Now, beyond all odds, I understand what maternal means. We are building a family.

#IN MEMORY OF….

Zoe is researching early childhood development, thinking about how she can be part of Marca Hope's growth. There is a knock on the door that startles her. She answers and no one is there. She looks down and sees a box addressed to her.

Oh, the baby stuff is here! Wow, it's early.

Once she brings the box into the kitchen and opens it, she sees a clear container labeled *Inmate Property*. Inside is a slightly folded object that appears to be a photo of Ruby Blue and Marcus. Realizing this, Zoe opens the box and pulls out the photo, showing Ruby Blue smiling from ear to ear with Marcus hugging her and smiling with his eyes. Smooth.

> *I should get this picture framed and surprise Ruby Blue and Marca Hope with a memorial for Marcus. I know I have a nice frame somewhere in this house and I'll order some silk roses, pink, just like he would have wanted.*

* * *

Zoe gently knocks on Ruby Blue's door, careful not to wake Marca Hope. She opens the door and pokes her head inside, saying, "Ruby Blue, I have something to show you." Ruby Blue, confused, follows Zoe down the hall into the living room.

Instantly, tears of joy fall as she sees the first photo they took together, next to the pink silk roses. Emotionally, she says, "How did you get this, Zoe?"

Zoe leaves the room, then returns. "From this box of his things sent from the prison he was transferred to. Sorry I didn't have you open the box first. I just wanted to do something special for you and Marca Hope. In memory of Marcus."

Ruby Blue embraces Zoe. "Thank you so much. This means the world to me. I never thought I'd see him again and now I can show Marca Hope who her daddy was. He won't just be a figment of her imagination."

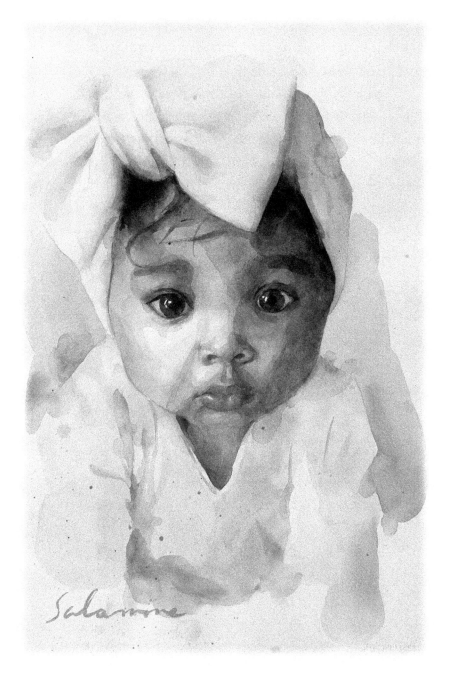

MARCA HOPE SMITH

#MARCA HOPE SMITH

We've got life and I'm feelin' mighty sassy. And just like my daddy would say, I'm mighty fine like aged wine. All my people gonna know that's me.

My name is Marca Hope Smith. But you can just call me Hope.

#AFTERTHOUGHT

They raised me. These two mighty women, a team—forces to be reckoned with—in that odd little house where we continue to live. We three changed that awful kitchen wallpaper one winter weekend.

My mama did her thing and was accepted into nursing school. She studied while Zoe hugged and played and disciplined and loved me. They both did—took turns, although, gratefully, Mama did most of the cooking.

She learned to love herself even in a world where your life can be taken away from you in a whisper; in a world where the only thing guaranteed is yesterday. She learned to love, and trust, those around her. Well, most anyway.

The Covid-19 pandemic eased, but death tolls were measured in millions. Some attempts to prepare for the next pandemic were discussed and even global Centers of Excellence set up, but we know that the threat increases as climate changes occur and wildlife habitats disappear and humans and the critters are forced to interact in new ways, creating more opportunities for viruses to jump between species. All interconnected.

After her graduation, Mama—Ruby Blue to some—and some of her classmates, started The Center for Strong Black Women. The Center focused exclusively on helping underserved Black women and their families, especially those facing difficult pregnancies. They hired teachers who taught parenting skills, and then involved the moms in ongoing coaching, women helping women. I participated in the programs and now am studying nursing as well.

We took care of Zoe when the dementia began to muddle her mind. While some people's brains lead them to anger as dementia grows, others become more and more kind. Zoe walked that second path. We got her a black-and-white, slow, and olding cat she named Nala, who snuggled with her many days as they rested in the sun. Zoe died peacefully in her beloved home—now ours—and surrounded by the two of us and other nurses from the Center.

And what did we collectively say? We said, "From Hardship to Hope: Don't stress the inevitable. Granny, you are missed. Know that we will always love you."

SOURCES

RACE, PREJUDICE, HISTORY, ACTIVISM

Alam, Rumaan. 2020. *Leave the World Behind*. New York: Harper-Collins.

Angelou, Maya. 2010. *I Know Why the Caged Bird Sings*. New York: Random House.

Baldwin, James. 1955. *Notes of a Native Son*. London: Penguin Books.

Baldwin, James. 2013. *Go Tell It on the Mountain*. New York: Vintage International.

Baldwin, James. 2013. *No Name in the Street*. New York: Vintage.

Baldwin, James, Steve Schapiro, John Lewis, and Gloria Karefa-Smart. 2017. *The Fire next Time*. Cologne, Germany: Taschen.

Bennett, Brit. 2022. *The Vanishing Half*. New York: Riverhead Books.

Braithwaite, Patia, Tiffanie Graham. May 25, 2023. *The Toll of Police Violence on Black People's Mental Health*. https://www.nytimes.com/interactive/2023/05/25/well/mind/black-mental-health-police-violence.html?searchResultPosition=6

Channing Brown, Austin. 2018. *I'm Still Here: Black Dignity in a World Made for Whiteness*. New York: Convergent Books.

Coates, Ta-Nehisi. 2015. *Between the World and Me*. New York: Spiegel & Grau.

Coates, Ta-Nehisi. 2019. *The Water Dancer*. UK: Penguin.

Cummins, Jeanine. 2020. *American Dirt: A Novel*. New York: Flatiron Books.

de Beauvoir, Simone and Bernard Frechtman. 2018. *The Ethics of Ambiguity*. New York, NY: Open Road Integrated Media, Inc.

Desmond, Matthew. 2016. *Evicted: Poverty and Profit in the American City*. New York: B\D\W\Y, Broadway Books.

Diangelo, Robin J. 2020. *White Fragility: Why It's so Hard for White People to Talk about Racism*. Boston: Beacon Press.

Eberhardt, Jennifer L. 2020. *Biased: Uncovering the Hidden Prejudice That Shapes What We See, Think, and Do*. London: Penguin Books.

Ellison, Ralph. 2015. *Invisible Man*. New York: Penguin.

Fanlund, Paul. April 7, 2021. *Listen More Than You Talk, and Other Advice on Racial Justice*. Madison, WI: Captimes.com.

Garvey, Marcus, and Robert Blaisdell. 2004. *Selected Writings and Speeches of Marcus Garvey*. Mineola, NY: Dover Publications.

Ginsberg, Maggie. January, 2021. "When Safer at Home Isn't." Madison, WI: *Madison Magazine*.

Glaude, Eddie S. 2021. *Begin Again*. London: Chatto & Windus.

Hansberry, Lorraine. 1960. *A Raisin in the Sun*. New York: Vintage.

Harris, Kamala. 2020. *The Truths We Hold: An American Journey*. New York: Penguin Books.

Harris, M A, Morris Levitt, Roger Furman, Ernest Smith, and Toni Morrison. 1974. *The Black Book*. New York: Random House.

Haws, Stephanie. Spring, 2021. "Finding a Voice Against All Odds." Madison, WI: *On Wisconsin*.

Hill, Fiona. 2021. *There is Nothing for You Here: Finding Opportunity in the Twenty-First Century*. New York: Mariner Books.

Hitchcock, Jeff. 2002. *Lifting the White Veil*. NJ: Crandall, Dostie & Douglass.

Holloway, Jonathan Scott. 2021. *The Cause of Freedom: A Concise History of African Americans*. New York, NY: Oxford University Press.

Irving, Deb. 2014. *Waking up White: And Finding Myself in the Story of Race*. Cambridge, MA: Elephant Room Press.

Johnson, George M. 2020. *All Boys Aren't Blue*. New York: Farrar, Straus and Giroux (BYR).

Jones, Kimberly, and Gilly Segal. 2019. *I'm Not Dying with You Tonight*. Naperville, IL: Sourcebooks Fire.

Kendi, Ibram X. 2017. *Stamped from the Beginning: The Definitive History of Racist Ideas in America*. New York, NY: Bold Type Books [Nation Books].

Lewis, John, Andrew Young, and Kabir Sehgal. 2021. *Carry On*. UK: Hachette.

Loewen, James W. 2008. *Lies My Teacher Told Me: Everything Your American History Textbook Got Wrong*. New York: New Press.

McWhorter, John H. 2017. *Talking Back, Talking Black: Truths about America's Lingua Franca*. New York, NY: Bellevue Literary Press.

Majors, Richard & Janet Billson. 1992. *Cool Pose: The Dilemmas of Black Manhood in America*. New York: Touchstone.

Morrison, Toni, 1987. *Beloved*. New York: Alfred A. Knopf.

Mott, Jason. 2022. *Hell of a Book*. New York: Dutton.

Noah, Trevor. 2016. *Born a Crime: Stories from a South African Childhood*. New York: One World.

Oluo, Ijeoma. 2019. *So You Want to Talk about Race*. New York, NY: Seal Press.

Perkins-Valdez, Dolen. 2022. *Take My Hand*. New York: Penguin.

Perry, Imani. 2018. *Looking for Lorraine: The Radiant and Radical Life of Lorraine Hansberry*. Boston, MA: Beacon Press.

Rankine, Claudia. 2020. *Just Us: An American Conversation*. Minneapolis: Graywolf Press.

Reich, Robert. May 8, 2023. *Why a New Progressive Era in America is Likely – in About 20 Years: Until then, Be Careful*. Robert Reich's newsletter. San Francisco, CA.

Roth, Philip. 2001. *The Human Stain*. New York, NY: Vintage Books.

Sellers, Bakari. 2020. *My Vanishing Country: A Memoir*. New York, NY: Amistad.

Smith, Clint. 2021. *How the Word is Passed*. New York, NY: Little, Brown.

Talking Black in America. n.d. WWW.youtube.com. Accessed June 14, 2021. https://www.youtube.com/watch?v=8QFpVgPl9tQ.

West, Cornel. 2017. *Race Matters*. Boston: Beacon Press.

Wilkerson, Isabel. 2016. *The Warmth of Other Suns: The Epic Story of America's Great Migration*. New York: Random House.

Wilkerson, Isabel. 2023. *Caste*. New York: Random House Trade Paperbacks.

Williams, P J. 1991. *The Alchemy of Race and Rights: Diary of a Law Professor*. Cambridge: Harvard University Press.

Wise, Tim. 2011. *White like Me: Reflections on Race from a Privileged Son: The Remix*. Berkeley, CA: Soft Skull Press.

NATIVE AMERICAN

Alexie, Sherman. 2017. *You Don't Have to Say You Love Me*. New York: Little, Brown.

Erdrich, Louise. 2021. *The Night Watchman: A Novel*. New York: Harper Perennial.

How to Grow a Three Sisters Garden. n.d. www.nativeseeds.org.

Kimmerer, Robin Wall. 2022. *Braiding Sweetgrass*. Minneapolis: Zest.

Momaday, N Scott. 2019. *House Made of Dawn*. New York: Harper Collins.

Orange, Tommy. 2018. *There There*. New York: Vintage.

Protecting Tribal Land, Preserving Natural Resources. www.wisconsinacademy.org. August 3, 2022. https://www.wisconsinacademy.org/magazine/summer-2022/initiatives-update/protecting-tribal-land-preserving-natural-resources.

Rolo, Mark Anthony. 2012. *My Mother Is Now Earth*. St. Paul, MN. Borealis Books.

INCARCERATION/CRIME/REHABILITATION/RESTORATIVE JUSTICE

Alexander, Michelle. (2010) 2020. *The New Jim Crow: Mass Incarceration in the Age of Colorblindness*. New York: New Press.

Betts, Reginald Dwayne. 2010. *A Question of Freedom: A Memoir of Learning, Survival, and Coming of Age in Prison*. New York: Avery/Penguin.

Butler, Shatki & World Trust. 2020. Healing Justice. Film. https://vimeo.com/395247138

Capote, Truman. (1965) 2013. *In Cold Blood*. New York: Modern Library.

Clauer, Joshua William and Judith Gwinn Adrian. 2021. *Walking the Line: There is No Time for Hate*. Milwaukee, WI: Henschel-HAUS.

DOC-1024 (Rev. 02/2009) DAI Policy #: 300.00.09. *Death of an Inmate*. Effective Date: 10/19/20.

Gwinn-Adrian, Judith, and DarRen Morris. 2014. *In Warm Blood: Privilege and Prison, Hurt and Heart*. Milwaukee, WI: Henschel-HAUS.

Hartman, Kenneth E. 2010. *Mother California*. New York: Atlas and Company.

Millar, Jackie, and Judith Gwinn Adrian. 2007. *Because I Am Jackie Millar*. Los Angeles: Golden.

Myers, Walter Dean, and Christopher Myers. 2019. *Monster*. New York, NY: Harperteen.

Raine, Adrian. 2013. *The Anatomy of Violence: The Biological Roots of Crime*. New York: Pantheon Books.

Rideau, Wilbert. 2011. *In the Place of Justice: A Story of Punishment and Deliverance*. New York: Vintage Books.

Stevenson, Bryan. 2019. *Just Mercy: A True Story of the Fight for Justice*. New York: Spiegel & Grau.

Stevenson, Bryan. 2014. TED talk: "We Need to Talk about an Injustice." https://www.ted.com/talks/bryan_stevenson_we_need_to_talk_about_an_injustice

PANDEMIC, ILLNESS, DEATH, DYING, GRIEVING

Gamio, Lazaro; Eleanor Lutz, and Albert Sun. May 11, 2023. "As Emergency Ends, a Look at Covid's U.S. Death Toll." https://www.nytimes.com/interactive/2023/05/11/us/covid-deaths-us.html?name=styln-corona-irus&region=TOP_BANNER&block=storyline_menu_recirc&action=click&pgtype=Interactive&variant=undefined

Gawande, Atul. 2014. *Being Mortal*. New York: Metropolitan Books.

Gupta, Sanjay. 2012. *Monday Mornings*. MA: Grand Central Publishing.

Jaouad, Suleika. 2022. *Between Two Kingdoms: A Memoir of a Life Interrupted*. New York: Random House.

Marley-Henschen, Holly. September 2022. "The Care Gap." *Madison Magazine*: Madison, WI.

Kalanithi, Paul. 2016. *When Breath Becomes Air*. New York: Random House.

Kubler-Ross, Elisabeth. 2005. *On Grief and Grieving*. New York: Scribner's.

Petrusich, Amanda. 2022. Review of "Talking about Grief with Anderson Cooper." *The New Yorker*, 30, 2022.

Roach, John. March 2021. "A Drawer Full of Masks." Madison, WI: *Madison Magazine*.

Roach, John. February 2022. "Enough Already." Madison, WI: *Madison Magazine*.

Russo, Richard. 2020. *Chances Are . . .* New York: Vintage.

Saunders, Gerda. 2017. *Memory's Last Breath: Field Notes on My Dementia*. New York: Hachette Books.

Tesfaye, Eva. April 17, 2021. "Life in The Roaring 2020s: Young People Prepare to Party, Reclaim Lost Pandemic Year." NPR https://www.npr.org/2021/04/17/987865318/life-in-the-roaring-2020s-young-people-prepare-to-party-reclaim-lost-pandemic-ye

Vora, Neil. April 2, 2023. "The Next Pandemic: 'The Last of Us' is right. Our warming planet is a petri dish." *The New York Times*.

Weller, Francis. 2015. *The Wild Edge of Sorrow: Rituals of Renewal and the Sacred Work of Grief*. Berkeley: North Atlantic Books.

OTHER

D'Egville, Angela. 2020. *Into the Lion's Den: A True Story Set in 1820 Africa*. Angela Patricia Tweddle, Monee, IL.

Ernaux, Annie, and Tanya Leslie. 2019. *Happening*. New York: Seven Stories Press.

Faulkner, William. 1929. *The Sound and The Fury*. New York: Vintage.

Frankl, Viktor E. 1959. *Man's Search for Meaning: The Classic Tribute to Hope from the Holocaust*. New York: Penguin Random House.

Fromm, Erich. 1956. *The Art of Loving*. New York: Harper & Row.

Gibrán, Kahlil. 1926. *Sand and Foam*. New York: Alfred A. Knopf.

Glaser, Gabrielle. 2021. *American Baby: A Mother, A Child, and the Shadow History of Adoption*. New York: Viking.

Gwinn Adrian, Judith. 2020. *Nancer the Dancer*. Milwaukee: HenschelHAUS.

Gwinn Adrian, Judith. 2018. *Tera's Tale*. Milwaukee: Henschel-HAUS.

Gutradt, Gail. 2015. *In a Rocket Made of Ice: The Story of Wat Opot, a Visionary Community for Children Growing up with AIDS*. New York: Vintage Books.

Hercules, Bob & Bruce Orenstein. 2010. *The Democratic Promise: Saul Alinsky & His Legacy*. (documentary)

Lawson, Michael L, and Vine Deloria. 1994. *Dammed Indians*. Norman: University of Oklahoma Press.

McRaney, David. 2022. *How Minds Change: The Surprising Science of Belief, Opinion, and Persuasion*. New York: Penguin Random House.

Quammen, David. April 23, 2023. *The Next Pandemic: Dead birds are falling from the sky*. nytdirect@nytimes.com.

Thích-Nhât-Hanh. 2013. *The Miracle of Mindfulness: An Introduction to the Practice of Meditation*. Boston, MA: Beacon Press.

Roach, John. May 2022. "Smoke and Mirrors." Madison, WI: *Madison Magazine*.

Sandburg, Carl. 1918. *Grass. Cornhuskers*. New York: Henry Holt & Co.

Saint-Exupery, Antoine de. 1943, *The Little Prince*. New York: Reynal & Hitchcock.

Sartre, Jean-Paul. 1948. *Existentialism is a Humanism*. London: Methuen & Co.

Towles, Amor. 2023. *The Lincoln Highway*. New York: Penguin.

Tremmer, Eleanor. June 9, 2021. "Is it Cultural Appropriation to use Drag Slang and AAVE?" https://www.babbel.com/en/magazine/cultural-appropriation-drag-slang-aave#:~:text=AAVE%2C%20or%20African%2DAmerican%20Vernacular,traced%20back%20to%20AAVE%20words.

ACKNOWLEDGMENTS

Our deepest appreciation to all who reviewed our manuscript and offered their generous comment. Special gratitude to those who have helped us make this book a pink, hold-in-your-hand reality: Kira, Phil, Neil, Neal, John, Elaine, Nicole, Martin, Carol, Joe, DarRen. And to our unwavering families. What more can we say but *muchas gracias!*

ABOUT THE AUTHORS
AND THE ARTIST

JUDITH GWINN ADRIAN, CO-AUTHOR

Judith Gwinn Adrian was born in Seattle and lived there to age seven when the family moved to Wilmette, Illinois. She completed BA and MA degrees in English at Luther College and Winona State University. Her Ph.D. is in Adult Education from the University of Wisconsin-Madison. After retiring from twenty-five years of teaching at Edgewood College, Judith became an author, working with Kira Henschel, HenschelHAUS. She lives in Madison, Wisconsin, with her husband and sturdy cat, Rufus. Her son and family reside in Minneapolis. Her birth daughter and granddaughter live in Massachusetts. Judith is a long-time volunteer with the JustDane Circles of Support, a reentry program for individuals as they are leaving prison.

More information at www.judithadrian.com

JAYLIN STUEBER, CO-AUTHOR

Jaylin Stueber is a Madison native who grew up on the East Side and is a Madison East High School alumna. Jaylin is also a PEOPLE and ITA (Information Technology Academy) alumna and has earned her Bachelor and Master of Social Work from UW–Madison. Currently she is the Behavioral Support and Engagement Counselor at Wingra School (students ages 5-14). Jaylin has always been passionate about working with youth and helping them stay on the right path to success, while also helping them achieve their short- and long-term goals. Additionally, she works to make an impact and stay connected with the Madison community by sitting on the Police Civilian Oversight Board (PCOB) as the vice-chair, and as a PCOB executive subcommittee member.

PHIL SALAMONE, ARTIST

Phil Salamone was born in Madison and raised in central Wisconsin. He graduated from the University of Wisconsin-Madison in fine arts and, seeking a classical understanding of painting from life, moved to New York to study at the Grand Central Atelier. After completing the three-year program, and studying at the Art Students League, he returned to Madison to paint and teach. In an effort to build a community, to learn from other artists, and to routinely practice painting from the figure, he rented a studio and began offering classes, workshops, and open studios. He teaches at both Madison College and his own school, the Atwood Atelier.

www.atwoodatelier.com

QUESTIONS FOR DISCUSSION

- How do we talk about racism with people who would benefit from the discussion, but are reluctant?

- How is our identity shaped by the ways others see and categorize us? How can we control this, if we can?

- How do we become more aware of our own implicit biases —our unexamined prejudices?

- When you hear about a police-involved shooting, how do you respond?

- How can we sidestep the culture wars, conflicts between groups with different cultural beliefs, ideals, and philosophies?

- Can respectful humor and authentic emotion be vehicles for initiating change?

- What is needed to move from a mindset of punishment to one of rehabilitation in our justice system?

- Do you see connections among over-population, climate change, and global pandemics? Next steps?

Printed in the USA
CPSIA information can be obtained
at www.ICGtesting.com
CBHW071547110424
6730CB00005B/18